First World War
and Army of Occupation
War Diary
France, Belgium and Germany

47 DIVISION
140 Infantry Brigade
London Regiment
8th (City of London) Battalion (Post Office Rifles)
1 August 1916 - 31 January 1919

WO95/2731/4

The Naval & Military Press Ltd
www.nmarchive.com
Published in association with The National Archives

Published by

The Naval & Military Press Ltd

Unit 10 Ridgewood Industrial Park,
Uckfield, East Sussex,
TN22 5QE England
Tel: +44 (0) 1825 749494

www.naval-military-press.com
www.nmarchive.com

This diary has been reprinted in facsimile from the original. Any imperfections are inevitably reproduced and the quality may fall short of modern type and cartographic standards.

Contents

Document type	Place/Title	Date From	Date To
Heading	140th Brigade. 47th Division. 1/8th Battalion London Regiment (Post Office Rifles) August 1916		
Heading	War Diary Of 8th Bn. London Regt (Post Office Rifles) from aug 1st to aug 31st 1916		
War Diary	Blangerval	01/08/1916	01/08/1916
War Diary	Villers L'Hopital	02/08/1916	04/08/1916
War Diary	Conte Ville	05/08/1916	05/08/1916
War Diary	Caours	06/08/1916	20/08/1916
War Diary	Mouflers	21/08/1916	21/08/1916
War Diary	Naours	22/08/1916	22/08/1916
War Diary	Beaucort	23/08/1916	23/08/1916
War Diary	Franvillers	24/08/1916	30/08/1916
Heading	War Diary Of 8th Batt. Lan. Regt. Month Of January, 1917 Vol 23		
War Diary	Devonshire Camp	01/01/1917	07/01/1917
War Diary	Halifax Camp	08/01/1917	13/01/1917
War Diary	Right Sector Hill 60 Sub Sector	14/01/1917	16/01/1917
War Diary	Railway Dugouts	19/01/1917	19/01/1917
War Diary	Railway Dugouts	20/01/1917	22/01/1917
War Diary	Right Sector Hill 60 Sub Sector	23/01/1917	26/01/1917
War Diary	Devonshire Camp	27/01/1917	31/01/1917
War Diary		01/02/1917	12/02/1917
War Diary		13/02/1917	18/02/1917
War Diary		18/02/1917	28/02/1917
Heading	War Diary Of 8th Batt Lan Regt. Month of March, 1917 Vol 25		
War Diary		01/03/1917	12/03/1917
War Diary		13/03/1917	28/03/1917
War Diary		29/03/1917	31/03/1917
Heading	1/8 Bn London Rgt June 1917		
War Diary		01/06/1917	07/06/1917
War Diary		08/06/1917	12/06/1917
War Diary		14/06/1917	30/06/1917
War Diary			
Operation(al) Order(s)	8th. Bn. London Regiment Order No. 67	02/06/1917	02/06/1917
Operation(al) Order(s)	8th. Bn. London Regiment (Post Office Rifles) Order No. 68	14/06/1917	14/06/1917
Operation(al) Order(s)	8th. Bn. London Regiment (Post Office Rifles) Order No. 69	16/06/1917	16/06/1917
Operation(al) Order(s)	8th. Bn. London Regiment (Post Office Rifles) Order No. 70		
Operation(al) Order(s)	8th Bn. London Regiment (Post Office Rifles) Order No. 71	29/06/1917	29/06/1917
Operation(al) Order(s)	For Battn The London Regiment Order No. 161	03/06/1917	03/06/1917
Miscellaneous	Barrage will be as shewn on map issued with Preliminary Instructions No. CGX a/25.5.17	25/05/1917	25/05/1917
Operation(al) Order(s)	140th Infantry Brigade. Operation Order No. 174	08/06/1917	08/06/1917
Miscellaneous	Second Army Offensive 8th. Bn. London Regiment Instructions Series I		
Miscellaneous	Fighting Dress		

Miscellaneous	South of Canal		
Miscellaneous	Establishment for (a) and (b)		
Miscellaneous			
Miscellaneous	Rations Water Bombs S.A.A.		
Miscellaneous	Second Army Offensive 8th. Bn. London Regiment Instructions Series II		
Miscellaneous			
Miscellaneous	Second Army Offensive 8th. Bn. London Regiment Instructions, Series IV	02/06/1917	02/06/1917
Miscellaneous	Medical Arrangements Reference Operation Orders No, 174	08/06/1917	08/06/1917
Miscellaneous	Wire Cutters (large) and Gloves, Hedging.		
Miscellaneous	Second army Offensive 8th Bn London Regiment. Series V		
Miscellaneous			
Map	Map No. 5.6.		
Miscellaneous			
Miscellaneous	Accompanying War Diary for June 1917	08/07/1917	08/07/1917
Map	Trench Dumps		
Map	Spoil Bank Sub-Sector		
Map			
Map	Barrage Beyond Blue Line During 2nd Phase		
War Diary	Ridge Wood	01/07/1917	03/07/1917
War Diary	Camp at M 6a. 5.8.	04/07/1917	08/07/1917
War Diary	Left Sub-Sector	09/07/1917	11/07/1917
War Diary	Left Sub Sector	12/07/1917	24/07/1917
War Diary	Carnarvon Camp	25/07/1917	31/07/1917
Operation(al) Order(s)	Operation Order No 127 by Lieut Col W.F. Mildren CMG DSO	03/07/1917	03/07/1917
War Diary		01/08/1917	25/08/1917
War Diary		26/08/1917	31/08/1917
War Diary		01/09/1917	17/09/1917
War Diary		18/09/1917	30/09/1917
Miscellaneous	Officer Commanding 6th Bn. Lon. Regt. 15th Lon. Regt.	28/08/1917	28/08/1917
Miscellaneous	Stores the Coys before moving.		
Miscellaneous			
Operation(al) Order(s)	Operation Order No 139 by Major J.E. Mayward	08/09/1917	08/09/1917
Miscellaneous			
Operation(al) Order(s)	Operation Order No 142 By Lt. Col. F. Mildren. CMG. DSO.	19/09/1917	19/09/1917
Miscellaneous			
Operation(al) Order(s)	Operation Order No 141 by Major F.G. Mayward 6th Lond on Regt	17/09/1917	17/09/1917
Miscellaneous			
Miscellaneous	to Batt. H.Q. by 12 near the 10th inst.		
Miscellaneous			
Operation(al) Order(s)	Operation Order No 138 By Major J.E. Mayward	07/09/1917	07/09/1917
Diagram etc	A G.		
Map			
Map	Hooge		
Miscellaneous			
Miscellaneous	Training.		
Miscellaneous	Schedule.		
Map	Map No. 5.6.		
War Diary	Support in Gavrelle Sector	01/10/1917	02/10/1917

War Diary	Beverley Camp	03/10/1917	05/10/1917
War Diary	Maroeuil	07/10/1917	07/10/1917
War Diary	Left of oppy Sector	10/10/1917	15/10/1917
War Diary	Reserve at Railway Cutting	16/10/1917	25/10/1917
War Diary	Maroeuil	26/10/1917	30/10/1917
War Diary	Maroeuil	01/11/1917	09/11/1917
War Diary		09/11/1917	12/11/1917
War Diary		13/11/1917	21/11/1917
War Diary		22/11/1917	27/11/1917
War Diary		28/11/1917	30/11/1917
War Diary		30/11/1917	30/11/1917
War Diary		13/11/1917	13/11/1917
War Diary		30/11/1917	30/11/1917
Miscellaneous	Headquarters 140th Infantry Brigade	04/01/1918	04/01/1918
War Diary	Bourlon Wood Sunken Rd.	01/12/1918	02/12/1918
War Diary		02/12/1918	03/12/1918
War Diary	Hindenburg Support Line	04/12/1918	04/12/1918
War Diary		05/12/1918	10/12/1918
War Diary	Bertincourt	11/12/1918	13/12/1918
War Diary	Hindenburg Support Trench	15/12/1918	15/12/1918
War Diary		16/12/1918	19/12/1918
War Diary	Bertincourt	21/12/1918	21/12/1918
War Diary	Mericourt	22/12/1918	31/12/1918
War Diary		01/12/1919	16/12/1919
War Diary		17/01/1919	31/01/1919
Miscellaneous		31/01/1919	31/01/1919

140th Brigade.

47th Division.

1/8th BATTALION

LONDON REGIMENT (Post Office Rifles)

AUGUST 1 9 1 6

284

Confidential.

WAR DIARY

OF

8th Bn. London Regt

(Post Office Rifles)

from Aug 1st to Aug. 31st. 1916.

285

Instructions regarding War Diaries and Intelligence Summaries are contained in F. S. Regs., Part II. and the Staff Manual respectively. Title pages will be prepared in manuscript.

WAR DIARY
or
INTELLIGENCE SUMMARY.
(*Erase heading not required.*)

Army Form C. 2118.

August 1916

Vol 18

Place	Date	Hour	Summary of Events and Information	Remarks and references to Appendices
BLANGERVAL	August 1st		Battalion moved by March Route to VILLERS L'HOPITAL.	
VILLERS L'HOPITAL	2-3		Battalion remained in Billets at VILLERS L'HOPITAL	
do.	4		Battalion moved by March Route to CONTEVILLE	
CONTEVILLE	5		do do CAOURS.	
CAOURS	6-10		Battalion remained in billets at CAOURS.	
do	11		do do. Took part in Brigade exercise.	
do	12		do do Took part in Brigade night exercise	
do	13		do do	
do	14		do do Took part in Brigade operations	
do	15		do do Took part in Brigade night operations	
do	16		do do Took part in Brigade Route March	
do	17		do do Took part in Brigade night operations	
do	18		do do	
do	19		do do Took part in Brigade Concentration march	
do	20		Battalion moved by March Route to MOUFLERS. Took part in Brigade Outpost Scheme en Route.	

286

Instructions regarding War Diaries and Intelligence Summaries are contained in F. S. Regs., Part II. and the Staff Manual respectively. Title pages will be prepared in manuscript.

WAR DIARY
or
INTELLIGENCE SUMMARY.
(Erase heading not required.)

Army Form C. 2118.

August 1916

Place	Date	Hour	Summary of Events and Information	Remarks and references to Appendices
MOUFLERS	Aug 21		Battalion moved by march Route to NAOURS.	
NAOURS	22		do do BEAUCORT.	
BEAUCORT	23		do do FRANVILLERS.	
FRANVILLERS	24-26		Battalion remained in billets at FRANVILLERS.	
do	27		do do Reinforcements of 40 O.R joined the Battalion.	
do	28-30		Battalion remained in billets at FRANVILLERS. Casualties for month NIL	

[signature] Major
for Lieut Col:
8th Bn London Regt
(Post Office Rifles)

T2134. Wt. W708—776. 500000. 4/15. Sir J. C. & S.

287

288

Vol 23

WAR DIARY

OF

8th Batt. Lan. Regt.

MONTH OF JANUARY 1917.

Instructions regarding War Diaries and Intelligence Summaries are contained in F. S. Regs., Part II. and the Staff Manual respectively. Title Pages will be prepared in manuscript.

WAR DIARY

~~or~~

~~INTELLIGENCE SUMMARY~~

(Erase heading not required.)

Army Form C. [illegible]8.

Place	Date	Hour	Summary of Events and Information	Remarks and references to Appendices
Devonshire Camp	1-1-17 to 7-1-17		Battalion remained in Divisional Reserve	
Halifax Camp	8.1.17		Battalion moved into Brigade Reserve relieving 21st Bn London Regt. Major W.B. Vince M.C. on his return from a Course in England assumed command of the Battalion	
	9.1.17		Battalion remained in Reserve	
	10.1.17		do do Sec Lts Rodgers & Benstead proceeded to join Heavy Branch Machine Gun Corps	
	11.1.17		do do	
	12.1.17		do do Sec Lt Evans proceeded to join Heavy Branch Machine Gun Corps. 3 O.R. wounded	
	13-1-17		Battalion relieved 7th Bn London Regt on night 13/14th in Right Sector Hill 60 Sub Sector. 1. O.R. wounded	
Right Sector Hill 60 Subsector	14-1-17 – 15-1-17		Battalion remained in Sector. 1.O.R. wounded on 12th died of wounds	
	16-1-17		do do do a Bombardment of the German front line system to our immediate right & left was carried out by the Corps artillery in conjunction with Divisional artillery. Bombardment started with 5 minutes intense at 7.30 am. & continued deliberate the remainder of the day. The Germans retaliated between 5.30 pm – 7.30 pm. Two O.Rs killed. Sgt Coombes & 4 O.Rs wounded	
	17-1-17		Battalion remained in Sector. 1 O.R. killed. The following officers from 14th London Regt joined for duty:– Sec Lts Wilson, Buchanan, Hyslop, Fraser & Will	
	18.1.17		Battalion was relieved on night 18/19th by 7th London Regt & moved into SUPPORT. 1. O.R wounded. The following officers from 14th London Regt reported for duty.– Sec Lts Hawkins Gibson & King. Draft of 93 other ranks "trained" arrived	
Railway dugouts	19.1.17		Battalion remained in SUPPORT. 2 O.Rs wounded. Sec Lts Bennett, Broatch & Wilkes from 14th London Regt joined for duty.	

2449 Wt. W14957/M90 750,000 1/16 J.B.C. & A. Forms/C.2118/12.

290

Army Form C. 2118.

Instructions regarding War Diaries and Intelligence Summaries are contained in F. S. Regs., Part II. and the Staff Manual respectively. Title Pages will be prepared in manuscript.

WAR DIARY
~~or~~
~~INTELLIGENCE SUMMARY~~

(Erase heading not required.)

Place	Date	Hour	Summary of Events and Information	Remarks and references to Appendices
Railway Dugouts	20-1-17		Battalion remained in Support. 1 O.R. wounded	
	21-1-17		do do do. Sec Lt Rayden proceeded to join Heavy Branch Machine Gun Corps.	
	22-1-17		Battalion relieved 7th London Regt. on night 22/23rd. 1 O.R. killed	
Right Sector HILL 60 Sub Sector	23-1-17		Battalion remained in Sector. Second day of bombardment of enemy front line system. Five minutes intense at 9.30am & deliberate during the day. Enemy retaliation comparatively slight and generally on left Company. Sec Lt WILL wounded. Sgt Allen killed. C.S.M. Cannon & 7 ORs wounded. 23rd Division raided enemy trenches on our right at 9.30 pm.	
	24-1-17		Battalion remained in Sector	
	25-1-17		do do. Draft of 36 ORs "trained" received	
	26-1-17		do do. do 63 ORs do do. Battalion was relieved by 20th London Regt on night 26/27th & moved into Divisional Reserve. 2 ORs wounded on 23rd, died of wounds	
Devonshire Camp	27-1-17 to 31-1-17		Battalion remained in Reserve	

[signature]
Major
Cmdg 8th London Regt
(Post Office Rifles)

2449 Wt. W14957/M90 750,000 1/16 J.B.C. & A. Forms/C.2118/12.

291

Army Form C. 2118

WAR DIARY
or
INTELLIGENCE SUMMARY.
(Erase heading not required.)

Instructions regarding War Diaries and Intelligence Summaries are contained in F. S. Regs., Part II. and the Staff Manual respectively. Title pages will be prepared in manuscript.

Vol 24

Place	Date	Hour	Summary of Events and Information	Remarks and references to Appendices
			1/8th Bn. London Regt.	
	Feb.			
	1-2.		Batt. remained at DEVONSHIRE CAMP in Divisional Reserve.	
	3.		Batt. relieved 24th Bn. London Regt. in Support in CANAL Sub-Sector.	
	4		Batt. remained in support. Major F.D. Balfour attached to 15th Bn. London Regt. for duty. Capt. H.H. King attached to 7th Bn. London Regt. Draft of 1 O.R. received.	
	5-6.		Batt. remained in Support.	
	7.		Batt. relieved 15th Bn. London Regt. in LEFT SUB-SECTOR on night 7th/8th Feb. 1 O.R. wounded.	
	8.		Batt. remained in Left Sub-Sector. Draft of 7 O.R. received. 4 O.R. wounded	
	9.		Batt. remained in Left Sub-Sector. 4 O.R. accidentally wounded by explosion of detonator of a new German Rifle Grenade ("Granatenwerfer")	
	10.		Batt. remained in Left Sub-Sector. 1 O.R. killed and 4 wounded.	
	11.		Batt. remained in Left Sub Sector. 1 O.R. killed, 2 died of wounds, 2 wounded.	
	12.		Batt. relieved night 12th/13th by 15th Bn. London Regt. and moved into	

Support

T2134. Wt. W708—776. 500000. 4/15. Sir J. C. & S.

Instructions regarding War Diaries and Intelligence Summaries are contained in F. S. Regs., Part II. and the Staff Manual respectively. Title pages will be prepared in manuscript.

WAR DIARY
or
INTELLIGENCE SUMMARY.
(*Erase heading not required.*)

Army Form C. 2118.

Place	Date	Hour	Summary of Events and Information	Remarks and references to Appendices
	Feb.			
	13.		Batt. remained in Support. 1 O.R. wounded.	
	14		Batt. remained in Support.	
			2Lts. H.E. Hawkins, J Hyslop, and C.F.S. Wilkes posted to 14th Bn. London Regt., and proceeded to join that Batt.	
	15.		Batt. remained in Support.	
	16.		Batt. relieved 15th Bn. London Regt. in Left Section Canal Sub-Sector on night 16th/17th. Casualties 1 O.R. wounded.	
	17.		Batt. remained in Left Sector.	
			During night 17th/18th, an enemy raiding party consisting of 29 men attempted to raid our lines on extreme right of Section, (I 34. d. 20. 60) but were repulsed. The enemy retired leaving one dead in our trenches. Two dead and two prisoners were also left in trench occupied by 7th Bn. London Regt., a little further to the right. Our casualties as the result of the raid were 2 O.R. wounded.	
	18.		Batt. remained in Left Section. Draft of 20 O.R. received.	

293

Army Form C. 2[illegible].

Instructions regarding War Diaries and Intelligence Summaries are contained in F. S. Regs., Part II. and the Staff Manual respectively. Title Pages will be prepared in manuscript.

WAR DIARY
or
INTELLIGENCE SUMMARY

(Erase heading not required.)

Place	Date	Hour	Summary of Events and Information	Remarks and references to Appendices
	Feb.			
	18.		One O.R. Killed.	
	19.		Batt. relieved by 6th Bn. London Regt. on night 19th/20th, and moved into Divisional Reserve at DEVONSHIRE CAMP. Casualties O.R. 1 killed and 10 wounded including R/S/M. J.H. Clarke attached to Batt. for instructional purposes.	
	20.		Batt. remained at DEVONSHIRE CAMP.	
			The 6th Bn. London Regt. raided the enemy trenches (from Left Section in which we were relieved on the 19th) and succeeded in taking 1 Officer and 114 other ranks prisoners and capturing 5 machine guns. Our Batt. Stretcher Bearers were attached to 6th Bn for this occasion and lost ~~assisted in the raid losing~~ 1 O.R. killed.	
	20-26		Batt remained in Divisional Reserve at DEVONSHIRE CAMP.	
			2Lt A. WOOLLEY and 5 O.R. joined Batt. from BASE on 25th Feb.	
	27.		Batt relieved 21st Bn. London Regt. in Right Section, HILL 60 Sub-Sector on night 27th/28th – moving to YPRES by train	
	28.		Batt. remained in Right Section. Heavy bombardments on Brigade Front by Artillery of both sides commenced at 9.30 p.m. and lasted for about one hour. Casualties other ranks 2 killed 5 wounded.	

A Blice[?] Major.
O/C. 8th Bn. London Regt.
(Post Office Rifles)

294

Vol 25

WAR DIARY

OF

8th Batt. Lan. Regt.

month of MARCH, 1917.

295

1

Army Form C. 2118

Instructions regarding War Diaries and Intelligence Summaries are contained in F. S. Regs., Part II. and the Staff Manual respectively. Title Pages will be prepared in manuscript.

WAR DIARY
~~or~~
~~INTELLIGENCE SUMMARY~~
(Erase heading not required.)

Place	Date	Hour	Summary of Events and Information	Remarks and references to Appendices
	March 1.		Bn. remained in Right Section, Hill 60. Sub-Sector.	
	3-4		Bn. remained in Right Section. Inter-Company relief carried out night 3rd/4th. Casualties 1 O.R. killed on 4th.	
	5.		Bn. remained in Right Section. Draft received – 2Lt. W.B. Will, 2Lt. C.H. Walker, 2Lt. W.J. James and 14 other ranks.	
	6		Bn. remained in Right Section: Casualties 1 O.R. killed.	
			The following Officers were posted to 1/14th Bn. London Regt. and proceeded to join that Battalion:– 2Lts. W.L. Wilson, L.R. Fraser, B.H. Gibson, L.D. Bennett, R.W. Broatch.	
	7.		Bn. remained in Right Section. Casualties 1 O.R. wounded.	
			Inter Company relief carried out night 7th/8th.	
	8-9.		Bn. remained in Right Section. Casualties 1 O.R. killed on 9th.	
	10.		Bn. remained in Right Section. Casualties 1 O.R. accidentally wounded.	
	11		Bn. remained in Right Section. Casualties – A/Capt A.L. Horsburgh wounded.	
			Inter Coy. relief carried out night 11/12 March.	
	12.		Bn. remained in Right Section. Casualties 1 O.R. wounded.	

2449 Wt. W14957/M90 750,000 1/16 J.B.C. & A. Forms/C.2118/12.

296

2

Instructions regarding War Diaries and Intelligence Summaries are contained in F. S. Regs., Part II. and the Staff Manual respectively. Title Pages will be prepared in manuscript.

WAR DIARY
or
INTELLIGENCE SUMMARY
(Erase heading not required.)

Army Form C. 21[illegible]

Place	Date	Hour	Summary of Events and Information	Remarks and references to Appendices
	March 13.		Bn. remained in Right Section. Casualties 1 O.R. accidentally wounded. 2Lt. A. Woolley evacuated sick to England.	
	14.		Bn. remained in Right Section. Casualties 1. O.R. killed.	
	15.		Bn. remained in Right Section. Bn. relieved on night 15/16th by 20th Bn. London Regt., and moved back into Divisional Reserve at DEVONSHIRE CAMP. Casualties 1 O.R. killed 2 O.R. wounded.	
	16-17		Bn. remained at DEVONSHIRE CAMP. March 17th - 2nd anniversary of Battalion's departure for France.	
	18-20.		Bn. remained at DEVONSHIRE CAMP. A/Major F.D. Balfour transferred to 15th Bn. London Regt. 20/3/17.	
	21.		Bn. relieved 24th Bn. London Regt. in CANAL RESERVE CAMP (H27b Sh.28NW) near DICKEBUSCH ~~on night 21/22~~. during afternoon.	
	22-24		Bn. remained in CANAL RESERVE CAMP. Draft received on 24th. - Capt. A.S. THOMAS and 29 other ranks. Casualties 2 O.R. killed and 1 wounded.	
	25-28.		Bn. remained in reserve at CANAL CAMP.	

2449 Wt. W14957/M90 750,000 1/16 J.B.C. & A. Forms/C.2118/12.

297

Instructions regarding War Diaries and Intelligence Summaries are contained in F. S. Regs., Part II. and the Staff Manual respectively. Title Pages will be prepared in manuscript.

WAR DIARY
or
INTELLIGENCE SUMMARY
(Erase heading not required.)

Army Form C. 2118.

Place	Date	Hour	Summary of Events and Information	Remarks and references to Appendices
	March			
	29.		Bn. relieved 15th Bn. London Regt. in Left Section CANAL sub-sector on night 29/30.	
	30.		Bn. remained in Left Section. Enemy heavily shelled the ~~night of~~ Bn. Support area ~~[illegible]~~. Casualties. 8 O.R. killed 12 wounded.	
	31.		Bn. remained in Left Section.	

B. [illegible] Lt Col.
Commanding 8th Bn. London Regt.
(Post Office Rifles)

2449 Wt. W14957/M90 750,000 1/16 J.B.C. & A. Forms/C.2118/12.

298

Index..

SUBJECT.

No.	Contents.	Date.
	1/8 Bn London Rgr June 1917	

(56,425). Wt.24,741--161. 2000. 11/20. Gp.164. A.&E.W.

299

1/

Instructions regarding War Diaries and Intelligence Summaries are contained in F. S. Regs., Part II. and the Staff Manual respectively. Title Pages will be prepared in manuscript.

WAR DIARY
or
~~INTELLIGENCE SUMMARY~~

(Erase heading not required.)

Army Form C. 2118.

1/8th Bn London Regt. (Post Office Rifles)

WO 95/28

Place	Date	Hour	Summary of Events and Information	Remarks and references to Appendices
	June 1-2		Batt. remained at DOMINION CAMP	
	3.		Batt. relieved 18th Bn. London Regt in SPOIL BANK Sub-Sector night 3/4.	
			Casualties Wounded 1 O.R.	
	4-6.		Batt. remained in Sub. Sector.	
			Dumps and trenches etc. were prepared for forthcoming operations. Our artillery carried out an incessant bombardment on enemy's trenches by day, and on his communications by night. Enemy retaliation for the bombardment was slight.	
			Casualties 4th wounded 1 O.R., 5th wounded 2 O.R., 6th wounded 2 O.R.	
	7.		Batt. was in position for attack by 1.30 AM.	
			An account of the Operations from 3.10 AM to 7 AM is attached.	
			Battalion consolidated in their final objective during the remainder of the day.	
			Batt. Headquarters moved to position near the DAMM STRASSE at 9.15 AM.	
			About 9 pm. the enemy artillery opened out very strongly and a counter attack was anticipated by the garrison holding the trenches immediately in front of us. The enemy were dispersed by our artillery and machine Gun fire, while preparing for attack.	
			The	

2449 Wt. W14957/M90 750,000 1/16 J.B.C. & A. Forms/C.2118/12.

300

2/

Army Form C. 21

WAR DIARY
or
INTELLIGENCE SUMMARY
(Erase heading not required.)

Instructions regarding War Diaries and Intelligence Summaries are contained in F. S. Regs., Part II. and the Staff Manual respectively. Title Pages will be prepared in manuscript.

Place	Date	Hour	Summary of Events and Information	Remarks and references to Appendices
	June		The remainder of the night was comparatively calm.	
	8.		Batt. remained in same position during day. Fierce artillery duel took place during evening. At 11.30 p.m., Batt. moved back to O.G. 1 and 2 with Headquarters at NORFOLK BANK.	
	9-11		Battalion remained in O.G. 1 and 2.	
	12		At 12.30 AM. Batt. relieved 7th Bn. London Regt. in Left Front Line with Headquarters at WHITE CHATEAU.	
			Battalion was relieved by 11th Bn. Royal West Kent Regt. at 11.15 p.m. and moved to CHIPPEWA CAMP.	
			Total casualties for period June 7-12:-	
			Officers Killed. { Capt. A.T. Davies (Welsh Regt. attd)	
			2Lt E. Henderson	
			Wounded { Capt. C.B. Fenwick (Northern Cyclist Batt. attd.)	
			2Lt M.W. Peters	
			Lt T.C.H. Berry (Welsh Regt. attd.)	
			2Lt J.D. Billham (R.W. Fusiliers attd.)	
			2Lt E.H. Foster. (Welsh Regt. attd.)	
			2Lt W.J. James.	
			Other Ranks. Killed 39. Died of Wounds 13. Wounded 172.	
			Wounded and missing 2. Missing 2.	

2449 Wt. W14957/M90 750,000 1/16 J.B.C. & A. Forms/C.2118/12.

301

3.

Army Form C. 2118.

Instructions regarding War Diaries and Intelligence Summaries are contained in F. S. Regs., Part II. and the Staff Manual respectively. Title Pages will be prepared in manuscript.

WAR DIARY
or
INTELLIGENCE SUMMARY

(Erase heading not required.)

Place	Date	Hour	Summary of Events and Information	Remarks and references to Appendices
	June 14.		Batt remained at CHIPPEWA CAMP.	
	15		Batt. marched to the CAESTRE Area and billeted for the night in and around St SYLVESTRE CAPPEL.	
	16.		Batt. marched to LYNDE.	
	17–27		Batt. remained at LYNDE. During this period the Companies were reorganized and refitted. On 26th a Divisional Aquatic Gala was held on the Canal at BLARINGHEM. The open Relay race was won by the Battalion team.	
	28.		Batt. marched to METEREN area and billeted outside village of METEREN.	
	29.		Batt. marched to RIDGE WOOD and billeted in tents and bivouacs there.	
	30.		Batt. remained in RIDGE WOOD. Drafts were received during month as follows:- 10 other ranks – 5th June. 4 other ranks – 10th June. 2 other ranks 18th June 12 other ranks – 19th June.	

2 Lt

2449 Wt: W14957/M90 750,000 1/16 J.B.C. & A. Forms/C.2118/12.

302

4

Army Form C. 2118

WAR DIARY
or
INTELLIGENCE SUMMARY
(Erase heading not required.)

Instructions regarding War Diaries and Intelligence Summaries are contained in F. S. Regs., Part II. and the Staff Manual respectively. Title Pages will be prepared in manuscript.

Place	Date	Hour	Summary of Events and Information	Remarks and references to Appendices
	8		2 Lt J. S. McKenzie and 6 other ranks 25th June. 1 other rank 26th June. Lt Col. L. E. de Vesian joined Battalion from 2/8th Bn. London Regt. on June 18th, and assumed command on June 28th vice Lt Col. A. Maxwell attached to 23rd Bn. London Regt.	
	2/7/17		L. E. de Vesian Lt Col. Commanding 1/8th Bn. London Regt (Post Office Rifles)	

2449 Wt. W14957/M90 750,000 1/16 J.B.C. & A. Forms/C.2118/12.

SECRET

Copy No. 2

8th Bn. London Regiment

Order No. 4[illegible]

Ref. 28 N.W.

2nd June 1917

1. 8th Bn. London Regt. will relieve 18th Bn. London Regt. in SPOIL BANK Sub-Sector on night 3/4th June.

2. Bn. will be disposed as follows:-

LEFT FRONT	D Coy.
RIGHT FRONT	C "
LEFT SUPPORT	B "
RIGHT SUPPORT	A "
Bn. Hqrs.	NORFOLK BANK.

3. One Guide per platoon, 1 Guide per Lewis Gun and 1 for Hqrs. from 18th Bn. will be at the point where cross country track crosses ECLUSE TRENCH, I.32.a.8.4 at 11.30 p.m.

4. Coys will move off in Platoons at 200 yards distance with connecting files, in order C, D, B, A, HQ. at intervals of 8 minutes between Coys; leading platoon passing entrance to Camp G.24.a.0.5. at 8.30 p.m. Wandering Guides will be provided on the route, which will be the CROSS COUNTRY TRACK.

5. Lewis Gun Limbers will be at meeting place of Guides at 11.0 p.m.

6. Dress - Fighting Order.
Rations for the 4th will be carried on the man.
Further orders as to issue of Bombs etc will be circulated.

7. Advance party consisting of Works Officer, Bombing Officer, A/R.S.M., C.S.M's, Sig. Sgt. Pioneers and Bn. Storekeepers will parade at Orderly Room at 3.30 p.m.

8. Limbers for Camp Kettles, Coy Mess Stores as required in line and Hqrs. Stores will be at Camp Q.M. Stores at 7 p.m.

9. Officers valises will be dumped at Camp Q.M. Stores by 7 p.m.
Packs, Greatcoats and Caps will be dumped at Q.M. Stores OUDERDOM before 11 a.m. Greatcoats will be dumped separately and care will be taken that nothing is left in the pockets.

10. Completion of relief will be reported to Bn. Hqrs. by code word "BOISDINGHEM."

Copies to:

1. File	10. C.O.
2. War Diary	11. Adjt.
3. 40th Inf. Bde.	12. B.O.
4. 18th Bn. Lon. Regt.	13. T.O.
5-9 Coys	14. QMR.

[signature]
Lt. & A/Adjt.
for O.C. 8th Bn. London Regt.
(Post Office Rifles)

SECRET

5th Bn. London Regiment
(Post Office Rifles)

Copy No. 2

Order No. 68

14/6/17

Ref. Map HALEBROUCK. 5A.

1. 8th Bn. London Regt. will proceed to LYNDE in two marches
(a) CHIPPEWA CAMP to CAESTRE AREA on the 15th inst.
(b) CAESTRE AREA to LYNDE on the 16th inst.
Transport including baggage wagons will proceed with the Batt.

2. Bn. will parade at 5.10 p.m. in column of route on KEMMEL – RENINGHELST ROAD facing N.W. Head of column at T roads 200 yards North of Z in ZEVECOTEN. Order of march – Band, Hqrs, A, B, C, D Coys, Transport

3. Billetting party will meet the Staff Captain at Area Commandants Office CAESTRE at 5 p.m. 15th June. The Qmr. will issue necessary instructions.

4. Dress – F.M.O. without packs and steel helmets. Waterproof sheets will be [illegible] inside the flap of the haversack which will be carried on the back.
Pack and steel helmets will be clearly marked and dumped separately outside Qmr. Stores by 10 a.m. These will be reissued on arrival at LYNDE.
Officers valises will be dumped at QMR. Stores by 12 noon.
One Mess box per Coy and 2 for Echelon C will be placed on Mess Cart at QMR. Stores at 4 p.m.

5. Lewis Gun limbers, Cookers and Water Cart will be ready to move at 4.15 p.m.

[signature]
Lt. + A/Adjt.
for O/C 1/8th Bn. Lon. Regiment
(Post Office Rifles)

Copy to
1. File
2. War Diary
3. 140 Inf. Bde
4. C.O.
5. Sec. in C.
6. Adjt.
7. O.C. A Coy
8. " B
9. " C
10. " D
11. W.O. + B.O.
12. T.O.
13. QMR.
14. R.S.M.

305

SECRET 8th Bn London Regiment (Post Office Rifles) Copy No 2

Order No 69

16/6/17

Ref. Map - HAZEBROUCK 5a

1. 8th Bn. London Regiment will march to LYNDE today. Order of March - Band, Hqrs, B, C, D & A Coys.

2. Bn will parade as follows:-
Band, Hqrs, B and A Coys on ST SYLVESTRE CAPPEL - HAZEBROUCK RD. facing South with head of column at Cross Roads half way between ST SYLVESTRE and LE BREARDE
C & D Coys will parade with head of column at same place on the second class road facing N.E.
A sufficient gap will be left between B and A Coys to allow C and D to move into their place when the Bn moves off.
Parade will be at 5.25 p.m.

3. Mess Cart will call for mess stores as follows:
A Coy 4 p.m. - Echelon C 4.10 p.m. - Hqrs 4.15 p.m. - B Coy 4.25 p.m.
C and D Coys 4.35 p.m.

4. Cookers will move with their Coys.

5. Chargers will be at Officers Mess at 4.45 p.m.

6. All water bottles will be carried full and will be filled at once.

7. Transport, less cookers, will move separately under orders from B.T.O.

[signature]
Lt & A/Adjt
for O/C 1/8th Bn. London Regt
(Post Office Rifles)

Copies to
1. File
2. War Diary
3. 140th Inf Bde
4. 7th Bn. Lon. Regt
5. C.O.
6. Sec. in C.
7. Adjt
8. O.C. A Coy
9. " B "
10 " C "
11 " D "
12 W.O. & B.O.
13 T.O.
14. QMR.
15. R.S.M

306

SECRET

8th Bn. London Regiment
(Post Office Rifles)

Copy No. 2

Order No. 40.

Ref. Map - HAZEBROUCK 5a

1. 140th Infantry Brigade will move on 28th inst to METEREN Area, on 29th to RIDGEWOOD Area and on 30th into SUPPORT of 142nd Infy. Bde in the Line

2. 8th Bn. will ~~parade~~ parade on WALLON CAPPEL - LYNDE Road facing N.E., head of column at entrance to A Coy's main billet at 6.~~25~~ am

3. Order of march - Band, Hqrs, C, D, A and B Coys, Transport. A distance of 200 yards will be maintained between D and A Coys.

4. Bn. will halt at 8.55 am. for half an hour. The rear half of the Bn. will then close up and will resume its distance when Bn. moves off. Haversack rations will be taken for consumption during this halt. Tea will also be provided.

5. Cookers will move on to parade with their Coys and will march as follows,- C. D + A Cookers behind D Coy and B Cooker behind Bn.

6. Water bottles will be carried full and will be filled tonight.

7. Instructions will be issued for billetting party later.

[signature]

Lt + A/Adjt
1/8th Bn. Lon. Regiment
(Post Office Rifles)

Copies to:-
1. File
2. War Diary
3. 140th Inf. Bde.
4. C.O
5. Adjt
6. O.C. A Coy
7. " B "
8. " C "
9. " D "
10 L.G.O.
11 T.O.
12 QMR
13 R.S.M.

307

SECRET

8th Bn. London Regiment
(Post Office Rifles)

Copy No. 2

Order No. 71

29/6/17

Ref. Map HAZEBROUCK 5A

1. 8th Bn will march to RIDGEWOOD today.

2. Bn. will parade at 5.10 p.m. on METEREN – LAMANCHE Road facing N., head of column outside C Coy Hqrs. Order of march – Hqrs, D, A, Band, B and C Coys. A distance of 200 yards will be maintained between the Band and B Coy.

3. All Transport except Cookers will move to new Transport Lines under B.T.O.
Cookers will move ~~on to parade with Coys and march behind Bn~~ behind their Coys.

4. Mess Cart will collect 1 mess box per Coy and Hqrs mess stores at 4.15 p.m.

5. Haversack rations will be taken. Shrapnel helmets will be carried on the man and will be issued this afternoon.

(Sgd) L.E.B. Jacob

Lt. & A/Adjt.
1/8th Bn. London Regiment
(Post Office Rifles)

Copies to:-
1. File
– 2. War Diary
3. 140th Inf. Bde
4. C.O.
5. Adjt.
6. O.C. A Coy
7. " B "
8. " C "
9. " D "
10. L.G.O.
11. T.O.
12. QMR.
13. R.S.M.

SECRET. 7th Battn The London Regiment Order No. 161. Copy No 4.

Ref Trench Map. ST. ELOI 1/5000 and attached map.

3/6/17

1\. (a) The 47th (Lon) Division will co-operate in an attack by the Second Army against the Messines-Wytschaete Ridge.

(b) 142nd Inf. Bde will attack immediately North and 140th Inf Bde will attack immediately South of the Ypres-Comines Canal.

(c) The attack of the 140th Inf Bde will take place in two phases. The final objective of first phase being the BLUE line and the final objective of the second phase being the BLACK line as shewn on attached map.

(d) The 8th and 7th Battns will conduct the attack in the first phase.

(e) Second phase will consist of advance by 15th and 6th Battns from BLUE to BLACK line at ZERO + 3 hrs. 40 mins.

2\. Objectives.

(a) The Battn will attack immediately South of the Ypres-Comines Canal with the 8th Battn on the right and a Battn of the 142nd Inf Bde on the left.

(b) Objectives of, and boundaries between Coys are shewn on attached map.

(c) A Coy will be responsible for dealing with the White Chateau. B Coy will detail moppers up for Canal Bank up to & including the Iron bridge.

3\. Assembly.

(a) Assembly positions are as shewn on map attached.

(b) All troops will be in position by 2 hours before ZERO.

4\. Consolidation

(a) Front line will be organised in best tactical position on or in front of Oak Switch.

(b) A support line will be consolidated in the neighbourhood of Oak Reserve.

(c) C Coy will dig posts from O.4 b. 2.8. to Canal at O.4 b. 5.2 & will be responsible for linking up with 142nd Inf Bde who are occupying Strong Point at O.4. b. 8.1.

(d) Immediately Oak Trench and Oak Support are taken the platoons of D & B Coys in Oak Trench less moppers up will advance as a further wave in rear of A and C Coys to Oak Reserve.

(e) All men of D & B Coys then remaining in Oak Trench & Oak Support will move up to reinforce Oak Reserve as soon as possible after the 15th and 6th Battns have passed through.

(f) D & B Coys will be prepared at any time to reinforce A & C Coys.

5\. Day of Attack.

Zero & day will be notified later.

309

6. Barrage.
Barrage will be as shewn on map issued with Preliminary Instructions No. CGX2 d/25.5.18.
All ranks will be warned to follow up the barrage as closely as possible.

7. Communications
(a) Further copies of maps for message reports are issued with these orders
(b) Information must be sent in as often as possible, situation reports being forwarded at every clock hour.
(c) 2/Lt P. W. Roots will take charge of Battn Forward Command Post.

8. (a) All orders will be destroyed by 1 hour before Zero.
(b) No diaries or letters will be taken by Officers or men in the attack.
(c) These orders are to be read in conjunction with Preliminary Instructions Nos: CGX1 to CGX4 already issued.

K P Perriatt
Capt & Adjt
1st Bn. The London Regt.

Copy No. 1 Filed
2 War Diary
3 HQ 40th Inf. Bde. by Runner
4 OC. 8th Battn
5 OC A Coy
6 " B "
7 " C "
8 " D "
9 Intelligence Officer
10 Medical Officer
11 QM & TO.
12 Adjutant
13. RSM.

310

SECRET.

Copy No. 5

140th INFANTRY BRIGADE.

Operation Order No.174.

8th June, 1917.

1. Interchange of Battalion positions in the Brigade Area will take place tonight in accordance with attached map.

2. 17th London Regt. will take over from portion of the 23rd London Regt. leaving O.G.1 and O.G.2 at 10 p.m.
   8th London Regt. will leave present positions at 10.30p.
   Subject to these times Officers Commanding 6th and 7th Battalions will arrange times mutually
   O.C., 7th London Regt. will arrange direct with 23rd Lon Regt. the relief of his platoons.

3. Headquarters, 6th and 7th Battalions WHITE CHATEAU, 8th Battalion NORFOLK ROAD. 17th London Regt. present 7th London Regt.Headquarters.

4. 140 M.G.Company and 140 L.T.M.B. will not move.

5. Code word for relief complete "THAT'S BETTER".

6. On relief, 23rd London Regt. will retire to billets in 142nd Inf.Bde. Area - S.P.8, RAT ALLEY and its vicinity.

7. ACKNOWLEDGE.

H Peel

Captain,
for Brigade Major, 140th Infantry Brigade.

Copy No.	1	File.
,,	2	War Diary.
,,	3	G.O.C.
,,	4	6th Lon.Regt.
,,	5	7th ,,
,,	6	8th ,,
,,	7	15th ,,
,,	8	140th M.G.Company.
,,	9	140 L.T.M.B.
,,	10	Staff Captain
,,	11	Signals.
,,	12	17th Lon.Regt.
,,	13	141st Inf.Bde.
,,	14	142nd ,,
,,	15	73rd ,,
,,	16	47th Division.
,,	17	O.C., 23rd Lon.Regt.
,,	18	Capt.Entwisle, 23rd,Lon.Regt.

311

Secret

Second Army Offensive

8th Bn. London Regiment Instructions.

Series I

1. **Code for Days and Hours.**

In making reference to times before or after which operations will commence, the following nomenclature will be adopted in future.

(a) Referring to days.

'Z' day is the day on which operations take place.

One day before 'Z' = 'Y' Day
Two days before 'Z' = 'X' Day
Three days before 'Z' = 'W' Day
Four days before 'Z' = 'V' Day
Five days before 'Z' = 'U' Day

Days before 'U' day will be referred to as:-
'Z' - 6, 'Z' - 7, 'Z' - 8, etc.

One day after 'Z' = 'A' Day
Two days after 'Z' = 'B' Day
Three days after 'Z' = 'C' Day

Days after 'C' day will be referred to as:-
'Z' plus 4, 'Z' plus 5, 'Z' plus 6, etc.

(b) Referring to hours on 'Z' day.

Zero is the exact time at which operations will commence, and times will be designated in hours and minutes plus or minus from zero even if they encroach on 'Y' Day.

2. **Fighting Dress.**

(a) Haversack containing rations on braces.
(b) 2 Bombs.
(c) 3 Sandbags

312

Fighting Dress (contd)

(d) Each man of 1 rifle section per platoon will carry a pick or shovel.

(e) 2 Flares.

(f) 170 rounds S.A.A.

Distinguishing armbands will be worn as laid down in para. XXXII "Training of Divisions for Offensive action".

Packs, overcoats, waterproof sheets, etc. will be left behind.

Contact Aeroplanes.

(a) Two contact aeroplanes will be up from zero (if light enough) till 6 hours after zero. One will work North of the Canal and one South of it.

One contact aeroplane will be up from 10 hours after zero during the attack on the green line.

Contact aeroplanes will be distinguished by three broad white bands on the fusilage and by the attachment of a black board on the left lower plane, thus:

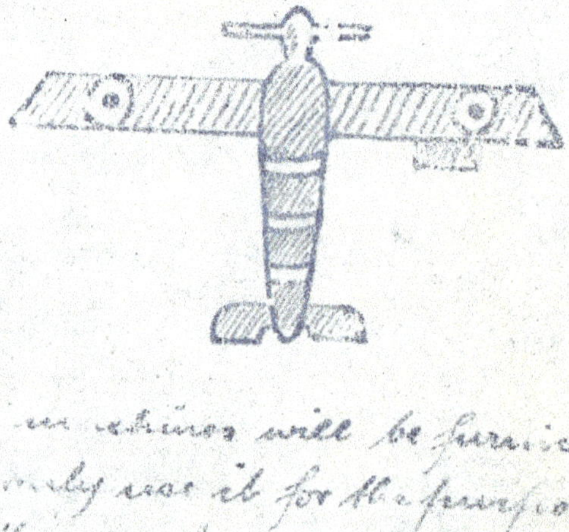

These machines will be furnished with wireless but will only use it for the purpose of reporting a counter attack or transmitting an infantry signal message calling for barrage.

Contact aeroplanes will call for flares by firing a white light and sounding a Klaxon horn.

Leading Infantry will light flares approximately at the following times:-

313

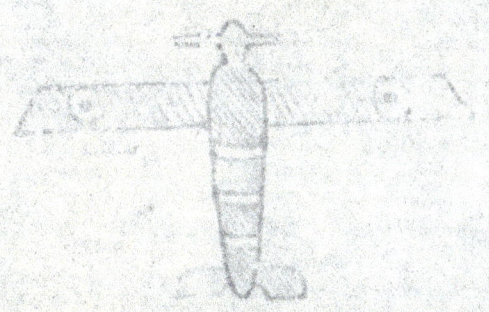

South of Canal

Zero plus 30'

" " 1 hr. 20'

" " 4 hrs. 30'

" " 5 hrs. 30'

Infantry must however ensure that the aeroplane is calling for flares before lighting up.

It is recognised that during confused fighting it is difficult for bodies of troops to know if they are actually the leading troops and it must not be assumed that flares show that there are no other troops in front.

Isolated bodies of troops out of touch on their flanks should light flares when called on to do so by aeroplane.

The colour of flares will be green.

(b) A wireless aeroplane will be up throughout the day from one hour after zero for the purpose of looking out for counter attacks. In event of a counter attack developing this machine will call on the artillery by the zone call and will warn the infantry by flares; a red flare will signify that the attack is North of the Canal and a green flare South of the Canal.

The zone call will give the position and direction of movement of the enemy's infantry and this information will be immediately communicated by the Artillery to the Infantry Brigadier concerned.

This machine will also transmit infantry messages calling for barrage.

4. Dumps.

(a) Advanced Brigade Dump at junction of OLD KENT ROAD and QUEENS ALLEY – O.3.6.05.95.

(b) Rear Battalion Dump. – O.3.6.6.8 where ESTAMINET LANE cuts the road.

314

Establishment for (a) and (b)

S.A.A.		40,000
Mills No. 5		2,000
" " 23		800
Very Lights 1"		10 boxes
" " 1½"		5 "
Aeroplane Flares		100
"P." Bombs		100
S.O.S Signals		25
Pistols 1"		4
" 1½"		2
Water	(galls)	100

(c) Trench Dumps

Right Battalion – O.3.b. 70.30 (approx.)
O.3.b. 50.25 "
O.3.b. 60.40 "

Establishment:-

S.A.A.		10,000
Mills No. 5		1,000
" " 23		500
Very Lights 1"		5 boxes
" " 1½"		2 "
Aeroplane Flares		50
"P." Bombs		25
Water	(galls)	50

5. Water

(a) Lock House

2 two-hundred gallon casks 400 galls

(b) Near First Aid Post in ESTAMINET LANE at I. 33.d.27.20

2 two-hundred gallon casks 400 galls

(c) Arundel House – In Tanks 300 "

(d) I. 33.c. 8.8 – 2 fifty-gallon tanks 100 "

(e) I. 33.c. 8.8 } Wells
I. 33.a. 1.2 }

315

The above water is for use on "Z" and subsequent days. The greatest care is to be taken of all petrol cans and rum jars. These must be returned to the dumps as soon as possible.

The importance of economising in water should be impressed upon all ranks.

6. Maps

Officers Commanding Coys are responsible that no orders diaries or letters, and only the specially issued maps of the German defences are taken into the trenches.

Treachery

All men should be warned against the possible instances of white flags and signs of surrender by the enemy.

Gas Helmets.

All gas helmets must be thoroughly examined before going into the line. When in the line men are to carry them at all times

9. Compasses

All Officers must carry compasses

10. Documents

All captured documents will be sent to Battalion Headquarters as soon as possible. If possible, a special party will be detailed to search dug-outs etc.

11. Bombs:

When objective is reached the 2 bombs carried by each man will be collected into central dumps for use of the Bombers. The position of such dumps to be pointed out to the Bombers.

316

12. Rations, Water, Bombs, S.A.A.

As far as possible rations, water, bombs and S.A.A. will be collected from casualties and stored in a convenient place to form a further reserve.

13. Petrol Cans

All water parties must bring down empty petrol cans with them. This is of great importance.

14. German Bombs and Gas Helmets

Specimens of these to be sent down to Battalion Headquarters.

15. Salvage

It is important that as much war material as possible should be returned. Small dumps should be formed to facilitate collection. Position of these dumps to be notified to Battalion Headquarters.

16. Observation Posts

Officers when selecting a line to "dig in" on after an attack must always bear in mind the paramount importance of including points from which good observation to their front can be obtained, in order to assist the work of our artillery in the next advance. They should be facing South East and South.

17. Rations.

2 days rations will be dumped in Battalion Headquarters in NORFOLK HOUSE Bunk

18. R.E. Dumps

Advanced R.E. Dump - LOCK HOUSE

19. Wounded

All slightly wounded men will carry their arms and equipment out of action. Anyone disobeying this order will have his name taken by the police and will be severely dealt with.

20. Public Money

Attention is called to G.R.O. 1911, para. 1. No public money is to be taken into action.

21. Stragglers Collecting Station & P. of W. Cage

Stragglers Collecting Station and Prisoners of War Cage will be established at H.20.c. 3.3.

All stragglers on arrival here will be examined by a medical officer and those found fit will be returned to 1st line Transport with an escort and be returned to their Units at first opportunity. Those found unfit will be sent to the nearest Field Ambulance.

317

Secret

Second Army Offensive

8th Bn. London Regiment Instructions

Series II

22. **Compasses**

To Instruction 9, Series I add:–
They will take bearings on their objective from their position of assembly. These bearings will be submitted to and checked at Bn. Hqrs. All Officers must know the variation of their compass.

23. **Rations**

Instruction 17 is cancelled.

(a) Supplies will be sent up to the line under Battalion arrangements. Greatest possible use to be made of pack transport and cross country tracks in order to avoid congestion on the roads, and reduce number of men required for carrying.

(b) All troops proceeding to the line will take up on the man rations for the next day in addition to the ordinary iron ration.

(c) 8th Bn. will consume on X day the iron rations at present stored in Brigade Dump SPOIL BANK.

Y and Z days rations will be stored in ARUNDEL HOUSE. These are full rations and will be dumped by W day.

Sandbags will be close to rations for distribution.

All water bottles are to be brought to the line full and instructions issued that water is to be used sparingly.

(d) On A day troops will use the iron ration carried on the man if it has not been possible to get rations up normally.

318

(c) Prior to W Day, Coys are held responsible that the biscuit portion of the iron ration (now stored in bulk at Battn. Hqrs.) is issued to and carried by all ranks

24. Dress

Officers will wear similar equipment to the men.

25. Very Pistols

These will be stored at Battn. Hqr. in readiness to be taken across to the captured trenches.

O.C. Coys who eventually occupy the new front line will ensure that these pistols are brought across so that they are available as soon as it is dark. These pistols are not to be taken across in the assault. A few will be kept in Reserve. All Very pistols will be returned to Battn. Hqrs before ZERO.

26. Dumps

2/Lt Appleton will be responsible for all Battn Dumps of Bombs, S.A.A., Rations &c.

27. Liaison Officer

2/Lt Hall will act as Liaison Officer between Brigade and Battn. and will report at Brigade Hqrs at ZERO minus 2 hours. He will also be responsible for marking out in the trenches the exact position of assembly of all Coys and Battn Forward Party.

28. Maxwell's Strong Point

The Strong Point at the junction of OAK ALLEY and OAK SUPPORT will be known as MAXWELL'S STRONG POINT

29. Machine Guns

One Section of 140th M.G.C. will proceed to the vicinity of OAK RESERVE about O.4.c.3.2. This Section will not move at ZERO but will proceed to their destination taking advantage of any lull in the barrage and will be ready to open fire as soon as possible to cover the consolidation of the BLUE LINE

30. Trench Names

The following names have been approved for new trenches, and name boards are being placed in position.

(a) Trench from CATFORD AVENUE to ESTAMINET LANE to be called } "CATFORD AVENUE" throughout.

319

(b) New trench from new portion of CATFORD AVENUE to OLD KENT ROAD to be called } "NEW CUT"

(c) New trench from OLD FRENCH TRENCH to the CANAL BANK which runs W of the Brickstack to be called } "ARUNDEL LANE"

31. <u>Bucket and Rope</u>

Each Watercart is to be equipped with a bucket and rope.

32. <u>Pack Transport.</u>

Units will be prepared to send forward rations, water and ammunition by Pack Transport in the event of the Bde being unable to approach the line to send carrying parties.

33. <u>Telescopic Sights.</u>

Telescopic Sights and rifles will not be taken into action but will be returned to Q.M. Stores before "X" day and will not be employed until conditions revert to those of stationary trench warfare.

320

SECRET

2.6.17

Second Army Offensive

8th Bn. London Regiment Instructions

Series IV

52. Removal of Wire in No-man's-Land

C and D Coys will be responsible for making gaps in the wire in front of the Sectors of O.B.1 from which they will assault. These gaps to be made on the night Y/Z. A careful reconnaissance of the wire to be removed will be made on night X/Y.

53. Up and Down Trenches.

Communication Trenches will be used as under:

Up (i) ESTAMINET LANE from SPOIL BANK to its junction with NORFOLK ROAD thence along NORFOLK ROAD

(ii) ESTAMINET LANE - WEST TERRACE - OLD KENT ROAD.

Down. FRONT LINE - ESTAMINET LANE (its junction with CATFORD AVENUE) - CATFORD AVENUE - NEW CUT - ANZAC CUT - OLD FRENCH TRENCH - ARUNDEL LANE.

Traffic Control Posts will be kept in position in O.B.1 and at each end of WEST TERRACE from ZERO - 1 hour to ZERO + 8 hours.

54. Messages

O.C. Coys are reminded that messages should be concise and as short as possible.

55. Distribution of Stores

The following Stores will be issued to Coys tomorrow morning at 10 a.m. and will be carried on the man. The B.O. will arrange issue.

S.A.A. - As laid down in Instruction No. 2 + 46

WEBLEY PISTOL AMMUNITION. - 36 rounds per Revolver.

S.A.A. BLANK - To the B.O.

MEDICAL ARRANGEMENTS REFERENCE OPERATION ORDERS NO, 178.

6th Battalion. 7th "	} at	WHITE CHATEAU.
8th Battalion.	at	SPOIL BANK.
15th Battalion.	at	GRENADE TRENCH.

Major.
Staff Captain.
140th Infantry Brigade.

8th June, 1917.

11/6/17

WIRE CUTTERS (large)
and
GLOVES, HEDGING

A	Coy	3	pairs
B	"	3	"
C	"	4	"
D	"	4	"
B.D		8	" (Reserve)

SECRET

Second Army Offensive.

8th Bn London Regiment.

Series V

56. Communications

(i) 4 Pigeons on "Z" day will be allotted to the Battalion

The "address to" and "address from" in pigeon messages will be the code name of the Unit concerned.

(ii) Flares. Coys are reminded that the small 1½ inch flares for communicating with contact aeroplanes should be placed in groups of 3 before lighting as they are difficult to distinguish from the rear.

(iii) Code. In order to shorten messages the following code will be used where applicable.

Have reached	Grace
Am advancing	Fry
Troops on Right held up	Hayward
" Left "	Hayes
" Right advancing	Hirst
" Left "	Hearne
" Right retiring	Hobbs
" Left "	Hitch
Am held up by enemy's barrage at	Blythe
" " " machine gun at	Rhodes
" " " wire at	Hardwick
Further bombardment required at	Gunn
Enemy are retiring at	Ranji
Enemy is now on line	Trumble
Enemy resisting strongly at	Noble
Am establishing post(s) at	Woolley
Am consolidating on line	Reeves
Enemy reinforcements moving up from	Dennett
Enemy massing for counter attack	Warner
Reinforcements wanted at	Abel
Am in touch with Bn on my Right	Barnes
" " " " Left	Denton
Dugouts bombed at	Jessop
Bombs wanted at	Briggs
Short of ammn	Spooner
Tanks have reached	Trumper
Tank disabled at	Trott
Tank required at	Tarrant
Casualties heavy	Carr
Casualties light	Champain.

324

56. Communications (contd)

IV. Overhearing by the enemy may be neglected as soon as the objective has been gained.

Messages may therefore be sent in clear by any means except Wireless and in this case the Signalling Sgt will use his discretion as to the relative importance of speed and secrecy.

V. Station Calls. After zero hour the signallers will use their normal Bn call i.e. t.H. Position Calls will not be used, either by units as addresses or by their signal offices in calling up.

VI. Small Air Balloons. F.O.Os. of 47th Divl Arty are being supplied with toy air balloons to which messages will be fixed and sent back in the event of failure of other means of communication and the wind being in a favourable direction.

Should these balloons be seen they should be gathered and their messages taken to the nearest Signal Station and forwarded as early as possible.

VII. Signalling to Balloons.

(a). During the forthcoming operations a balloon will be available to act as a receiving station for visual signals from units in the front line.

(b). Its position from "Z" Day onwards will be about 2000 feet above M.b.d. central by day; after 9 p.m. it will descend to about 1,500 feet.

(c). It will bear the following distinguishing marks:-

By day - 2 black flags 3 feet square carried on the balloon cable 200 feet below the balloon

By night - A lamp will give frequent flashes.

(d). Units will only use this balloon when all other means of communication have failed. It has no code call. A station will send its own call when wishing to call up the balloon.

325

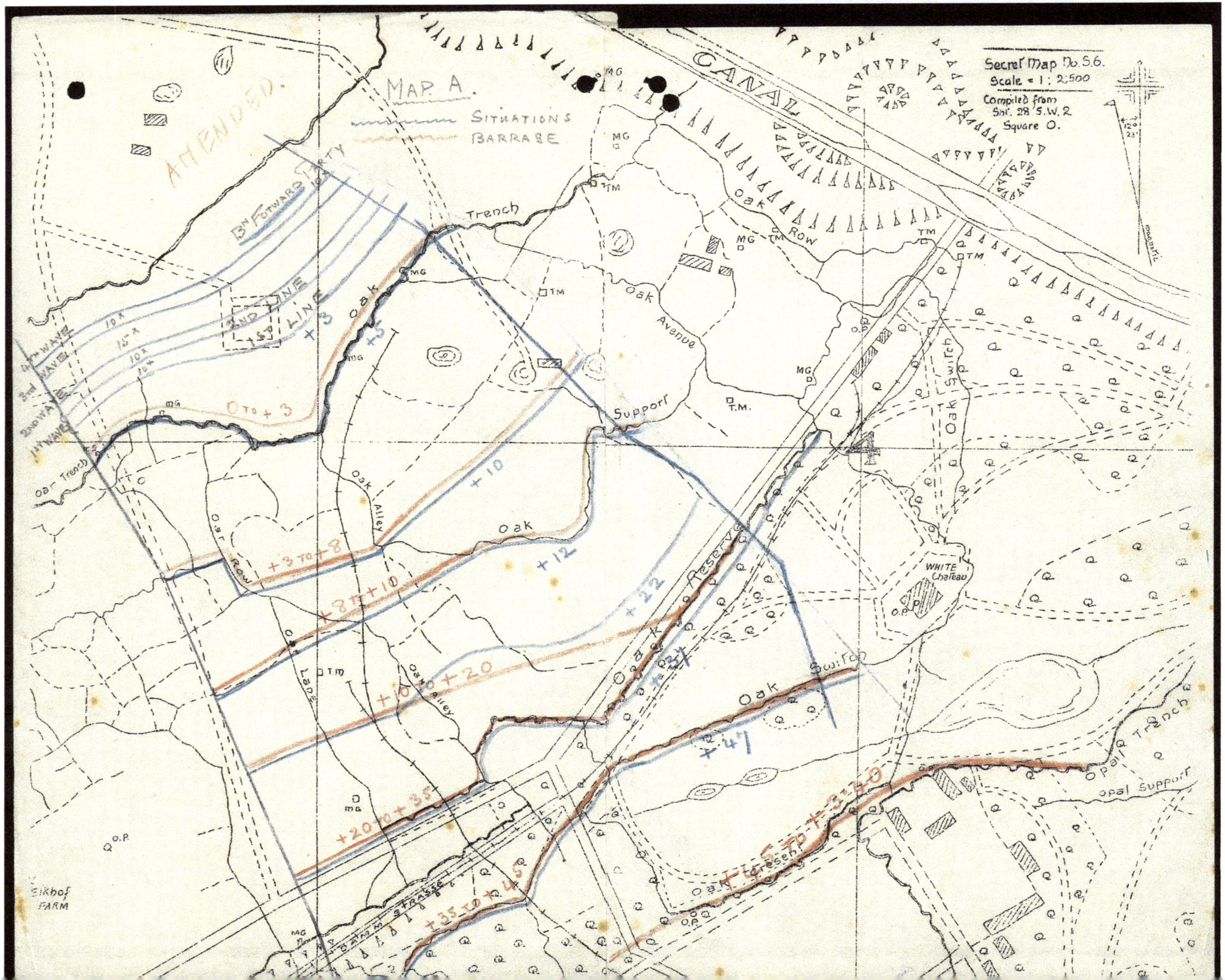

Secret Map No. 5.6.
Scale = 1 : 2,500
Compiled from Sht. 28 S.W. 2 Square O.
magnetic
MAP A.
SITUATIONS
BARRAGE
AMENDED.
CANAL
Bn Forward Party
2ND LINE
1ST LINE
1st WAVE
2ND WAVE
3rd WAVE
4th WAVE
0 to + 3
+ 3 to + 8
+ 8 to + 10
+ 10 to + 20
+ 20 to + 35
+ 35 to + 45
+ 45 to + 340
+ 3
+ 5
+ 10
+ 12
+ 22
+ 31
+ 47
Oak Row
Oak Avenue
Oak Support
Oak Trench
Oak Alley
Oak Lane
Oak Reserve
Oak Switch
Oar Trench
Oar Row
Opal Trench
Opal Support
Oak Crescent
DAMM STRASSE
WHITE Chateau
Eikhof FARM
O.P.
MG
TM

~~Accompanying War Diary for June 1917~~

140th Bde Operation Orders

166, 9, 7, 170, 1, 4, 5, 6, 8, 9

Miscellaneous Operation Orders.

8th Bn London Regt Operation Orders Nos. 66 – 71.

Miscellaneous Memos. and Orders in connection with 2nd Army Operations on June 7th.

Press Room 16

329

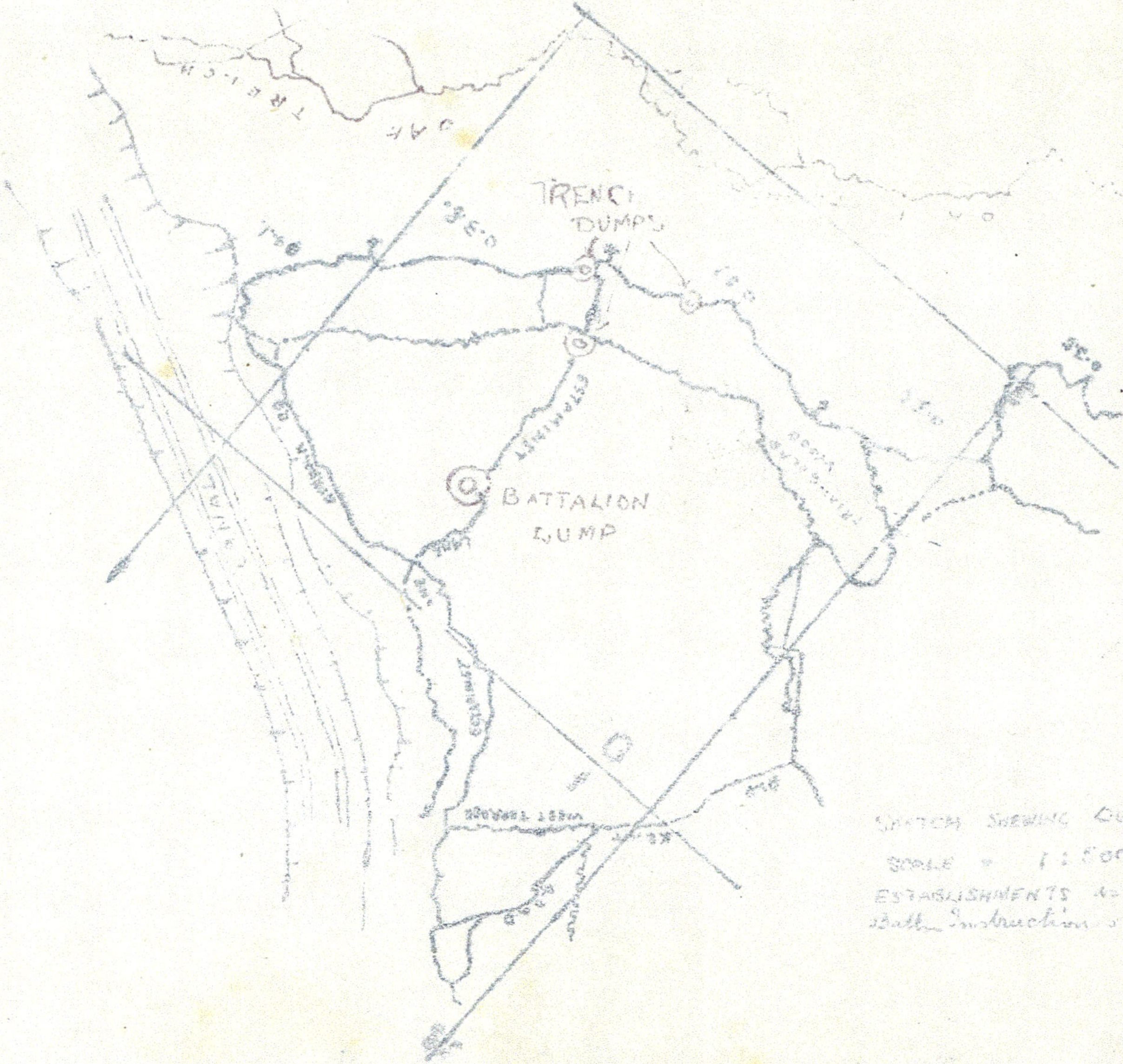

SKETCH SHEWING DUMPS

SCALE = 1:5000

ESTABLISHMENTS [illegible]

Batt. Instructions SERIES I PARA 4

330

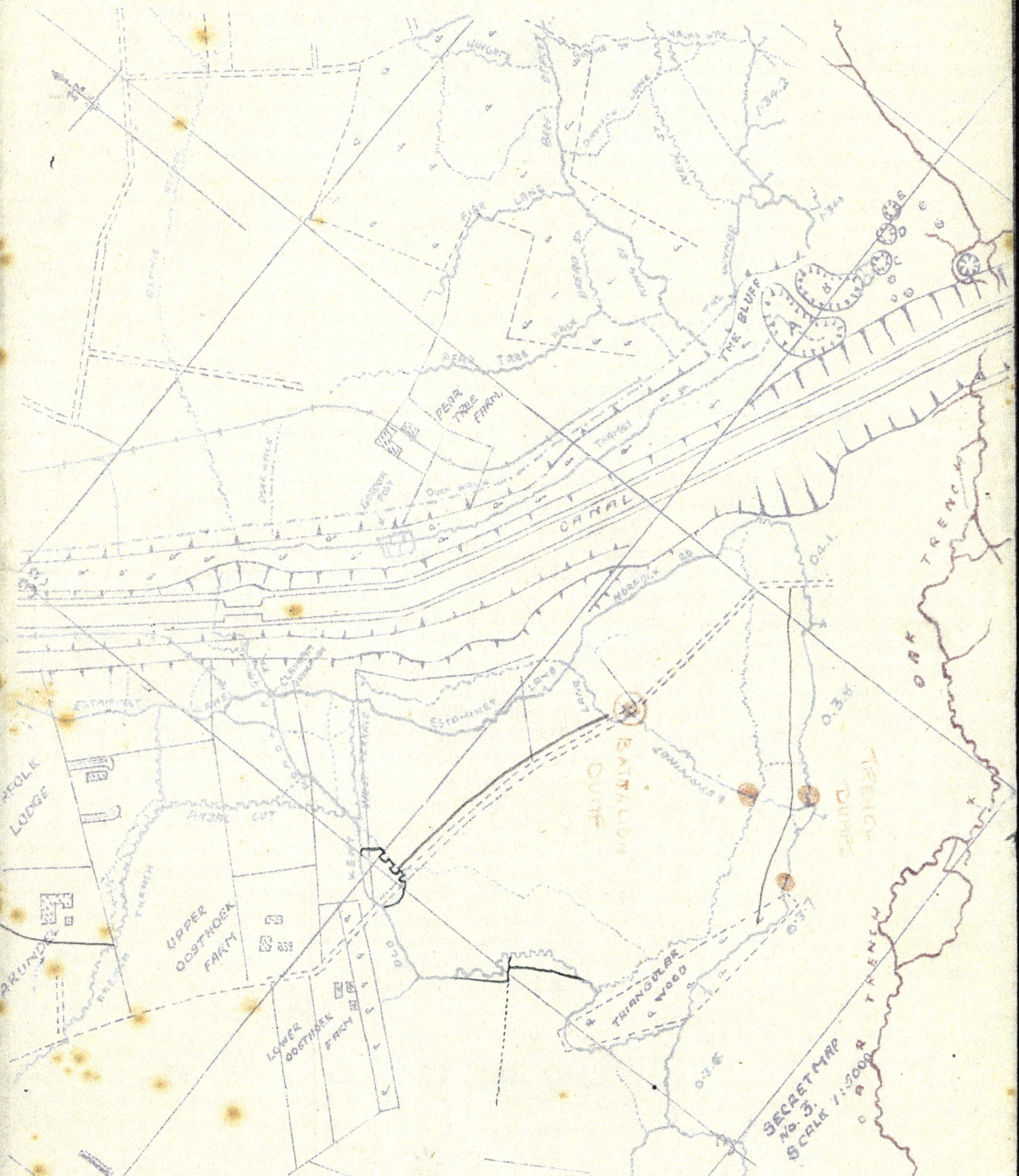

SPOIL BANK
SUB-SECTOR

12.4.17.

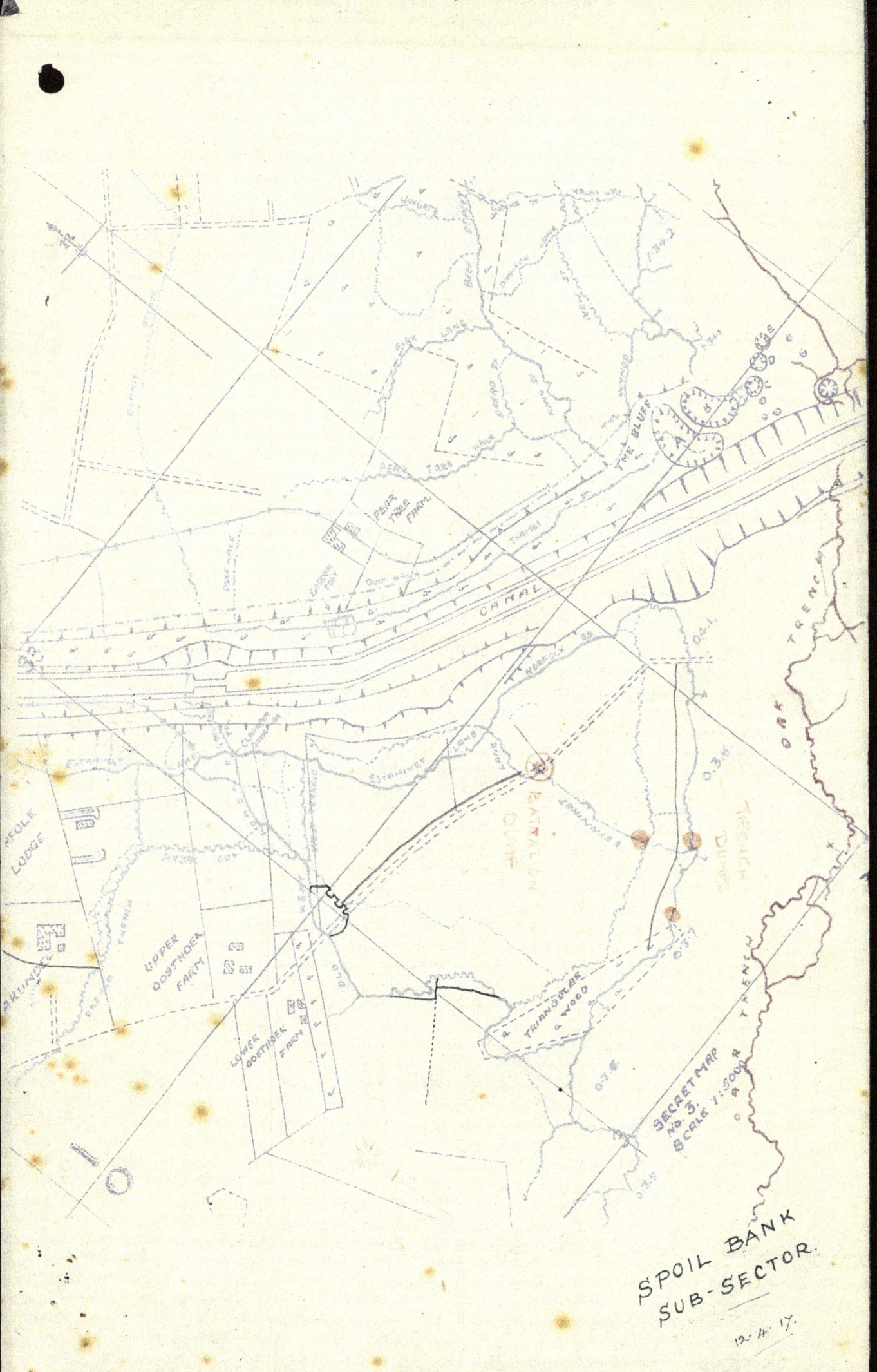

331

SECRET
8th
H.Q
17th
H.Q
H.Q
6th
7th
Battle Wood
10
Scale

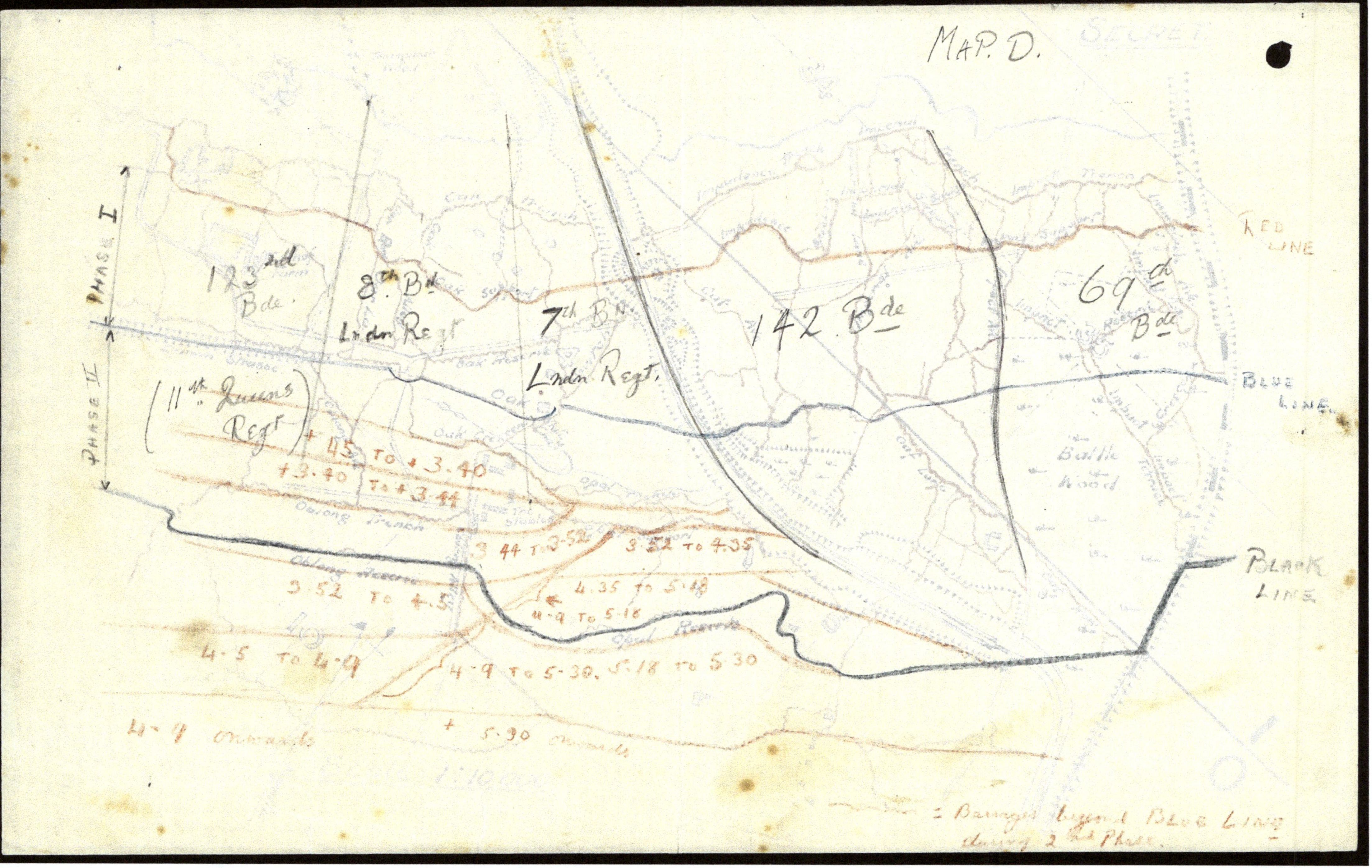
MAP. D.
SECRET
RED LINE
BLUE LINE
BLACK LINE
PHASE I
PHASE II
123rd Bde.
8th Bn Lndn Regt
7th Bn Lndn Regt.
142. Bde
69th Bde
(11th Queens Regt)
+ 45 to + 3.40
+ 3.40 to + 3.44
3.44 to 3.52
3.52 to 4.35
3.52 to 4.5
4.35 to 5.18
4.9 to 5.18
4.5 to 4.9
4.9 to 5.30. 5.18 to 5.30
4.9 Onwards
+ 5.30 Onwards
Oblong Trench
Battle Wood
= Barrage beyond Blue Line during 2nd Phase.

333

334

Instructions regarding War Diaries and Intelligence Summaries are contained in F. S. Regs., Part II. and the Staff Manual respectively. Title Pages will be prepared in manuscript.

1917

July

WAR DIARY

~~or~~

~~INTELLIGENCE SUMMARY~~

(Erase heading not required.)

Army Form C. 2

1/8th Bn. London Regt. (Post Office Rifles)

VK 29

Place	Date	Hour	Summary of Events and Information	Remarks and references to Appendices
RIDGE WOOD	July 1-3.	–	Bn. remained at RIDGE WOOD.	
			H.M. the King passed along road - HALLEBAST CORNER - VIERSTRAAT during his visit to Corps Area on the 3rd inst.	
			Draft of 18 other ranks received. Casualties 2 O.R. wounded.	
CAMP at M6a.5.8	4		Bn. moved to Camp at 28 M6a.5.8 on LA CLYTTE - RENINGHELST Rd.	
	5-7		Bn. remained in same billets.	
	8		Bn. relieved 23rd Bn. London Regt. in the left Sub-sector of Brigade Front, South of the CANAL, night 8/9, with Bn. Hqrs. in NORFOLK BANK. Casualties 2 O.R. wounded.	
Left Sub-Sector	9		The Brigade on the Right carried out a small attack with object of advancing its line. A patrol from Battalion followed up barrage with object of capturing machine gun believed to be in OBLIQUE TRENCH. One prisoner was obtained as result of raid. Casualties 4 O.R. wounded.	
	10.		Bn. remained in Sub-Sector.	
			Casualties 1 O.R. killed 7 O.R. wounded.	
	11.		Inter. Coy. reliefs took place night 11/12.	

2449 Wt. W14957/M90 750,000 1/16 J.B.C. & A. Forms/C.2118/12.

335

Army Form C. 2118.

WAR DIARY
or
INTELLIGENCE SUMMARY

(Erase heading not required.)

Instructions regarding War Diaries and Intelligence Summaries are contained in F. S. Regs., Part II. and the Staff Manual respectively. Title Pages will be prepared in manuscript.

Place	Date	Hour	Summary of Events and Information	Remarks and references to Appendices
Left Sub-Sector	July 12-13		Bn. remained in same positions.	
			Draft of 31 other ranks received 12th. Casualties 1 O.R. wounded 12th, 1 O.R. Killed 13th.	
	14		Bn. relieved by 6th Bn. London Regt. on night 14/15, and moved into Left Support with Headquarters in SPOIL BANK.	
			Casualties. Wounded Capt A.S. Thomas and 2Lt W.B. Will, Killed 6 O.R. wounded 6 O.R.	
	15-23		Bn. remained in Support.	
			Draft of 6 O.R. received on 15th.	
			Casualties 19th Killed 2Lt P.H. Cook, 2Lt G.E. Sanders, 5 O.R.s Wounded 10 O.R.s	
			Casualties 20th Killed 1 O.R. wounded 2 O.R.	
			2Lt R.P. Alsop joined Battalion for duty on 20th.	
			Casualties 21st Wounded 3 O.R.s	
			Draft of 7 O.R.s joined Batt. 22nd	
	24		Bn. relieved by 12th Bn. East Surrey Regt. on night 24/25, and moved back to CARNARVON CAMP 28 M.10 b.8.5	
			Casualties Wounded 2Lt H. Appleton, Killed 3 O.R. wounded 2 O.R.	

2449 Wt. W14957/M90 750,000 1/16 J.B.C. & A. Forms/C.2118/12.

336

Army Form C. 2118.

Instructions regarding War Diaries and Intelligence Summaries are contained in F. S. Regs., Part II. and the Staff Manual respectively. Title Pages will be prepared in manuscript.

WAR DIARY
or
INTELLIGENCE SUMMARY

(Erase heading not required.)

Place	Date	Hour	Summary of Events and Information	Remarks and references to Appendices
CARNARVON: CAMP	July 25-31		Bn. remained at CARNARVON CAMP. Draft of 4 O.R. received on 25th. The following Officers joined Battalion for duty 2Lt N.C. Holt, 2Lt E.G. Matthew, 2Lt H. King, 2Lt E.C. Knell. Draft of 12 O.R. joined Bn. on 30th.	

3/8/17.

[signature] Lt Col.
O/c 1/8th Bn. London Regt.
(Post Office Rifles)

2449 Wt. W14957/M90 750,000 1/16 J.B.C. & A. Forms/C.2118/12.

337

<u>SECRET</u> Operation Order No 127 <u>Copy No</u>

by

Lieut Col. W. F. Mildren CMG DSO

Commanding 6 "F" Battn Lon Regt

'R' TRENCH 3rd July 1917

1 <u>Re-allotment</u> The Divisional front will be reallotted from the night 3rd/4th July and will extend from O.11.a 20.20 to the KLEIN ZILLEBEKE ROAD at I.36.a 86.42

The front North of the CANAL will be held by the 141st Inf Bde, South of the CANAL by the 142nd Inf Bde.

The 140th Inf Bde will withdraw into reserve.

~~The 6th Battn after relief will become Divisional Works Battalion~~

2 <u>RELIEF</u> The Battalion will be relieved, tonight, by the 24th Battn London Regt as soon as that Battn is relieved in the front line. No guides will be required by the 24th Battn

3

4 <u>MOVE</u> As soon as the Battn is relieved it will move back to [illegible] ~~its former position in RIDGE WOOD~~. All movement will be by platoons at 100 yds interval.

5 <u>Trench Stores</u>. All Trench stores &c found in

327

Army Form C. 2118. 140/47

WAR DIARY
or
INTELLIGENCE SUMMARY
(Erase heading not required.)

1/8th Bn London Regt
August 1917.
Vol 30

Instructions regarding War Diaries and Intelligence Summaries are contained in F. S. Regs., Part II. and the Staff Manual respectively. Title Pages will be prepared in manuscript.

Place	Date	Hour	Summary of Events and Information	Remarks and references to Appendices
	Aug 1-7.		Batt. remained at CARNARVON CAMP. Draft of 9 OR. received on 7th	
	8.		Batt. moved to RIDGE WOOD. 2Lt T.R. GUY and 2Lt H. CLARKSON joined Batt. for duty.	
	9-11.		Batt. remained in RIDGE WOOD. Draft of 1 OR. received on 11th. Casualties 10th 1 OR. killed 3 wounded.	
	12		Batt. relieved by 12th Bn. Royal Sussex Regt., and moved to ASCOT CAMP, WESTOUTRE "A" area. Draft of 1 OR. received.	
	13-14		Batt. remained at ASCOT CAMP.	
	15		Batt. moved to the South TILQUES area by train, billeting in St MARTIN AU LAERT. Draft of 8 OR. received.	
	16-23		Batt. remained in billets at St MARTIN AU LAERT. During the period Battalion training including musketry was carried out. On 18th a Bde. Church Parade was held at LONGUENESSE at which the Bishop of Khartoum officiated. On the 22nd, the Bde. was inspected at LONGUENESSE by General Plumer commanding 2nd Army. Capt. A. S. Thomas M.C. rejoined Batt. from Base, and 2Lt D. O'Kell joined Batt. for duty 16th Aug.	
	24		Batt. proceeded by 'bus to WINNIPEG CAMP	
	25.		Batt. remained at WINNIPEG CAMP	

2449 Wt. W14957/M90 750,000 1/16 J.B.C. & A. Forms/C.2118/12.

338

Instructions regarding War Diaries and Intelligence Summaries are contained in F. S. Regs., Part II. and the Staff Manual respectively. Title Pages will be prepared in manuscript.

WAR DIARY
or
~~INTELLIGENCE SUMMARY~~
(Erase heading not required.)

Army Form C. 2[?]8.

Place	Date	Hour	Summary of Events and Information	Remarks and references to Appendices
	Aug 26.		Batt. relieved the 23rd Bn. London Regt. in the line night 26th, with Batt. Hqrs. on BELLEWARDE RIDGE.	
	27-30		Batt. remained in the line.	
			A post at J.8.a.9.2 (Sh. HOOGE 1/10000) was occupied by two sections of "D" Company on night 29/30, without opposition from the enemy.	
			Casualties during period 27/30:- 1 OR. killed 16 wounded on 27th. 1 OR. killed 12 wounded on 28th. 2 OR. wounded on 29th. 1 OR. killed 4 wounded on 30th. Following draft for Batt. proceeded to Corps Reinforcement Camp:- 2Lt. H.H. Tucker and 13 OR. on 27th.	
			Batt. was relieved on night 30/31 by 17th Bn. London Regt. On relief Batt. moved to YPRES, where it billeted for the night.	
	31.		Batt. moved to WINNIPEG CAMP.	

[signature]
Lt Col.
Commanding 1/8th Bn. London Regt.

2449 Wt. W14957/M90 750,000 1/16 J.B.C. & A. Forms/C.2118/12.

339

Army Form C. 2118.

Instructions regarding War Diaries and Intelligence Summaries are contained in F. S. Regs., Part II. and the Staff Manual respectively. Title Pages will be prepared in manuscript.

140/47

September 1917.

WAR DIARY
or
INTELLIGENCE SUMMARY
(Erase heading not required.)

8th Batt London Regt

Vol 31

Place	Date	Hour	Summary of Events and Information	Remarks and references to Appendices
	Sept. 1-7		Batt. remained at WINNIPEG CAMP.	
			Capt. H.H. King rejoined Batt. from attachment to 7th Bn. London Regt. on 3rd	
			2Lt. L.J. Hawes and 22 other ranks joined Battalion on 5th.	
			The Batt. was inspected by the Brigadier General commanding 140th Infy. Bde.	
	8.		Batt. relieved 1st Bn. Wiltshire Regt. in CANAL RESERVE CAMP (Southern portion) H.27 b. 6.4.	
	9		Batt. relieved 8th South Lancs. Regt. in dug-outs on WEST and SOUTH-WEST sides of ZILLEBEKE LAKE	
	10-16		Batt. remained in same positions. Casualties 2 Other Ranks killed on 12th; 6 other ranks wounded on 14th	
			Lt. Col. R.C. de Vesian proceeded to Hqrs. 18th Corps. Major W.B. Vince M.C. assumed command of the Battalion, on 16th.	
	17		Batt. was relieved by ~~a Batt. of the~~ 6th ~~ANZ~~ Australian ~~Infy.~~ Battn and moved to a camp at H 30. c. 5. 3.	

2449 Wt. W14957/M90 750,000 1/16 J.B.C. & A. Forms/C.2118/12.

358

Army Form C.2118.

Instructions regarding War Diaries and Intelligence Summaries are contained in F. S. Regs., Part II. and the Staff Manual respectively. Title Pages will be prepared in manuscript.

WAR DIARY
or
INTELLIGENCE SUMMARY
(Erase heading not required.)

Place	Date	Hour	Summary of Events and Information	Remarks and references to Appendices
	Sept 18.		Batt. proceeded to STEENVOORDE EAST area.	
	19.		Batt. remained in same billets.	
	20		Batt. proceeded to EECKE area. A draft consisting of 2Lt H. H. Tucker, 2Lt J. McGowan and 101 other ranks joined Batt.	
	21.		Batt. remained in same billets.	
	22		Batt. moved to 1st Army Area by train from CAESTRE Station, and billeted in and about CAPELLE-FERMONT near AUBIGNY (the detraining station). 2Lt R. Scott joined Batt.	
	23		Batt. remained in same billets. 2Lt Jh. Playfoot joined Batt.	
	24		Batt. relieved 22nd Bn. London Regt. at BEVERLEY CAMP - G.4.d. (Sh. 51B) *	
	25		Batt. relieved HAWKE Batt. (R.N. DIVN) in support ~~of Right Batt.~~ in Right Brigade Sector of new Divisional Front.	
			* The following officers joined Batt. on 24th 2Lts. E.C. Meredith, B.J. Fryer, E.S.W. Niles, R. Hainsworth.	
	26-30.		Batt. remained in support. 2Lt E. Day joined Batt. on 28th.	

B. Birnie Major.
o/c 1/8th Bn. London Regt. (Post Office Rifles)

2449 Wt. W14957/M90 750,000 1/16 J.B.C. & A. Forms/C.2118/12.

359

Secret

A866

Officer Commanding,
6th Bn.Lon.Regt.
15th do.

Herewith Dispositions of 8th Batt.Lond. Regt., together with maps.

BM/153/11,

G. R. Dub Captain,

28th August, 1917. Brigade Major, 140th Inf.Bde.

340

stores to Coys before moving.

V Relief Complete — OC Coys will advise Battn H.Q. by runner when relief is complete using word. "Once Again"

VI Officers Valises — Officers Valises will be stacked in Q.M. stores by 10·30 am

VII Packs — Packs will be ~~st~~ marked with number, name, & company & stacked in barn by Q.M.'s billet.

IX Dress — (a) Fighting Order, haversack on back.
(b) Ground Sheet.
(c) Cardigan
(d) 3 pairs socks to be carried on man.
OC Coys will render certificate to Orderly Room that all men are in possession of above.

(X) Cleanliness — All huts & surroundings will be left clean & tidy. OC Coys will render usual certificate to the Orderly Room.

XI Transport — Cookers will be ready to move by 10.45 am
Water carts " " 10.45 am
The Mess Cart & Medical Cart will be at the camp by 10.15 am.

G.H. Martin [illegible]

|| Dickebusch –
via: Kruisstraat – Warrington Road
cross country track – Shrapnel Corner
– MOATED GRANGE –

+ To guide Coys to their respective positions.

‡ Rationed & watered for one day.

(7) No other baggage other than the Camp kettles authorised for the use of Officers and other ranks will be carried on Omnibuses. Companies will arrange to take sufficient dixies ~~for immediate use~~ on arrival at destination.

(8) <u>Dress.</u> FMO with unexpended portion of the days ration

(9) <u>Transport</u> The transport will move via OTTAWA-BUSSEBOOM Road – junctions G21 a6.2 – G20 a4.4 – HOPOUTRE – ABEELE. OUDERDOM & RENINGHELST must not be entered. Keep north of these places using cross country tracks.
Starting Point Cross roads G24 c5.5 at 2.15 pm. 200 yards will be maintained between transport of units, horsed units, & other troops.

(10) Companies will notify Batt HQ when billetted in the new area

342

(11) All tents and surroundings will be left clean and tidy with tents brailed. Certificate to this effect will be rendered to the Adjutant.

H. T. Ordish
Capt. & Adj

Copies to: H.Q.
2 O/C A Coy
3 " B "
4 " C "
5 " D "
6 " T.O. "
7 " Q.M. "
8 " L.G.O.
9 " M.O.

343

Secret Operation Order No 139 Copy No

by

Major J. E. Maynard.

Commanding. 6th Batt: LONDON REGT.

DICKEBUSCH. 8-9-17

(1) Relief The Batt: will move into the front line and reserve tomorrow night. D Coy will relieve one Company of the 8th Border Regt: about J 8 C 5.6. and J 8 C 5.7. HQ Coy and A.B. & C Coys will relieve the 11th Cheshire REGT at HALFWAY HOUSE.

(2) Order of Relief.

2. B Coy will relieve B Coy 11th Cheshire REGT
3. C " " " A Coy & 1½ platoons C Coy "
1. A " " " D Coy 11th Cheshire REGT.
4. HQ "
5. D " " " – Coy 8th Border REGT.

(3) Move. A B. C. & HQ Coys companies will parade and move off in above order in small parties of 10 at 70 yards intervals, commencing at 4.15 pm. Guides will be met at Batt HQ HALFWAY HOUSE. X

D Coy will parade ^ and move off in small parties of 10 at 70 yards interval & meet guides at BIRR CROSS ROADS at 9.30 pm. D Coy will be relieved by the 18th Batt LONDON REGT. on

// These will proceed with the advance party.

½ secn of 7 Bde Signallers will proceed
w/ advanced pty.

326

Operation Order No 142
by
Lt Col: W F MILDREN. CMG. DSO
Commanding 6th Batt. London Regt
STEENVOORDE 19th Sept: 1917

1. MOVE The Battalion will move into billetts at EECKE tomorrow morning.

2. Parade The Battalion will be drawn up in Column of Route on the Road passing HQ. head of Column at "C" Coys billet - ready to move at am

3. Order of March.
HQ Coy
C "
Band
A Coy
B "
D "

4. Dress Full marching Order.

5. Tents + Bivouacs. All tents + bivouacs will be stacked by

Continued:–
Companies at convenient points by the road ready for transport at 6. am.

6. Valises Officers valises & mess stores will be ready for transport at   am.

7. Transport. The Transport will move in rear of the Battalion. The T.O will arrange to collect all tents & bivouacs and deliver them to the AN&H Company before the Battalion leaves.

8. Cleanliness. All billets will be left clean & tidy. O/c Coys will render a certificate to this effect to the Adjutant before leaving.

9. Companies will notify HQ, as soon as they are billeted in the new area.

Continued:—

Copies.

1. HQ
2. O/C A Coy
3. " B
4. " C
5. " D
6. TO & QM
7. LGO
8. M.O.

[illegible]
Capt & Adjt

OPERATION ORDER No 141
by
Major J. E. Maynard
Commending 6th LONDON REGT

H23C ~~CHATEAU SEGARD AREA~~ 17-9-17

(1) MOVE The Bn. will move by buses to the STEENVORDE EAST AREA on the 18th inst:

(2) EMBUSSING POINT H 14 b at 10.30. am.

(3) DEBUSSING POINT K32 d 5.0.

(4) ~~The~~ Bn Companies ~~will move by march route~~ to embussing point ~~by platoons~~ at 200 yards interval in the following order:- ~~and times~~

A Coy at 9. am
B " 9.10 "
C " 9.20 "
D " 9.30 "
HQ " 9.40 "

(5) Valises & Mess Boxes Officers valises & Mess Boxes will be stacked outside HQ tents 8.30 am.

347

Continued –
the night of the 10/11th details later.

LEWIS GUNS. OC A Coy will detail 4 Lewis guns and teams of 1 NCO + 4 OR for anti-aircraft duties // Guides will be met at HALFWAY HOUSE to guide these teams to their respective positions. The L.G. Officer will ensure that the teams are properly posted and understand their duties.

WORKING PARTIES

OC A Coy will detail permanent working parties as under.

(a) 1 NCO + 4 to take over pumping work in HQ tunnel.

(b) 2 NCOs + 8 to take over work at RIDGE HOUSE.

(c) 2 NCOs + 18 to take over work at DORMY HOUSE.

Guides for b + c parties will be met at HALF WAY HOUSE.

ADVANCE PARTY

2nd Lt. G.B. MARTIN. CSM SNOW, Corpl. SHARPE + 1 Signaller. Sgt THOMPSON, 1 NCO each from A.B + C Coys ~~and~~ Cpl: + 2 Runners LILLYWHITE will parade outside Orderly Room at 2.30 pm + proceed to take over for their respective companies. Copies of receipts for Trench Stores will be sent

#Kept at a convenient spot in the line [illegible] near HELL FIRE Corner [illegible] [illegible] [illegible] to be detailed by the L.90 [illegible] [illegible] until the picking up by I Coy [illegible] preceding to relief.

348

returned:-
to Batt: HQ by 12 noon the 10th inst:.

RELIEF COMPLETE
Coys will notify BATT: HQ on completion of relief using the words "WHAT HOPES".

Dress
BATTLE ORDER. All waterbottles will be filled by 3 p.m.

Transport
The Lewis Guns ~~of A B C~~ less "D" Coy Guns will be taken up to HALF WAY HOUSE & handed over to 33 Pte. Cpl: LILLYWHITE by ~~5.40 p.m.~~ ~~Those of B C companies by 7 p.m.~~ Those of D Company will ~~be at~~ ~~BIRR CROSS ROADS by 9.25 p.m. sharp.~~ The L.G.O. will supervise distribution of guns to companies.
The Mess Cart & Medical Cart will be at the Camp at 4 p.m. Limbers for dixies & fryers & Orderly room box will be at the Camp at 4 p.m.

Copy No. I Batt: HQ.
2 O/C A Coy
3 " B "
4 " C "
5 " D "
6 " QM & TO
7 " L.G.O.
8 " O/C 11th Cheshire Regt.

N. T. Ordish
Capt: & Adj:

1 By small parties of 10 at 50 yds interval using the S 3 track to SHRAPNEL CORNER.

349

(6) Billeting Party. 2nd Lt. COTTON & CQMS & Lcpl PARNELL will report to Staff Captain at the AREA COMMANDANTS OFFICE, RUE CARNOT, STEENVORDE at 9 am on the 18th inst: Party will meet the Battalion at debussing point to conduct to new billets.

(7) EMBUSSING & DEBUSSING ORDERS

(a) An omnibus seats 25 exclusive of the driver

(b) A seated lorry seats 20 exclusive of the driver

(c) Officers will be distributed among the buses.

(d) Strict discipline will be maintained during the move

(e) Troops will be distributed along the roadside as follows:-
6 groups of 25 men each to every 80 yards of road space

(f) Embussing should begin from the point of each section of the convoy, unless the embussing point is of sufficient length to fill all vehicles of a section simultaneously.

& ingredients for making tea

350

SECRET Operation Order No 138 Copy No

by

Major J. E. Maynard.

Commanding 6th Battn L'don Regt.

VANCOUVER CAMP 7-9-17

I Relief The Battn will relieve the 3rd Worcestershire Regt. at DICKEBUSCH tomorrow morning. HQ & A.B.D. Coys will be billeted at H33.a.7.8 & "C" Coy at CAVALRY CAMP (H27 d 8.3)

II. Order of Relief Coys will parade & move off by coys at 100 yds interval as under via MILLE-KAPELLEKEN FARM.

"C" Coy	move at	10.35 am
"A" "	"	10.40 am
"B" "	"	10.45 am
"D" "	"	10.50 am
H.Q.	"	10.55 am

III Lewis Guns The Lewis Gun Limbers will proceed to New Area under arrangements to be made by T.O.

IV Advance Party 2/Lt Cotton & 4 Q.M. Sgts & 1 N.C.O. to be detailed by R.S.M. for (H.Q.) will proceed to new camps & take over & arrange billets.

V Company Stores The R.S.M. will issue all company

351

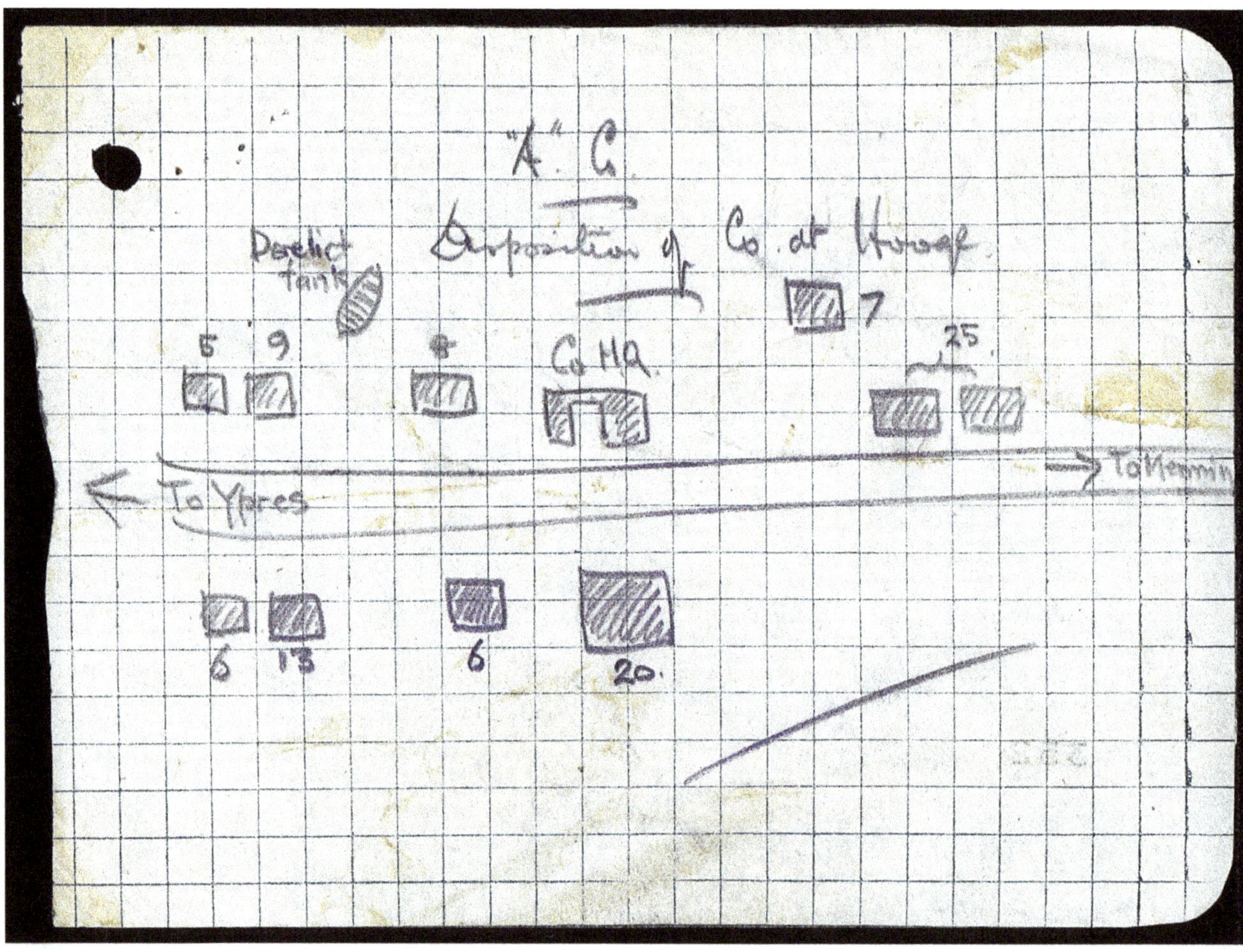

"A" Co.
Disposition of Co. at Hooge
Derelict tank
5
9
Co HQ
7
25
To Ypres
To Menin
6
13
6
20.

352

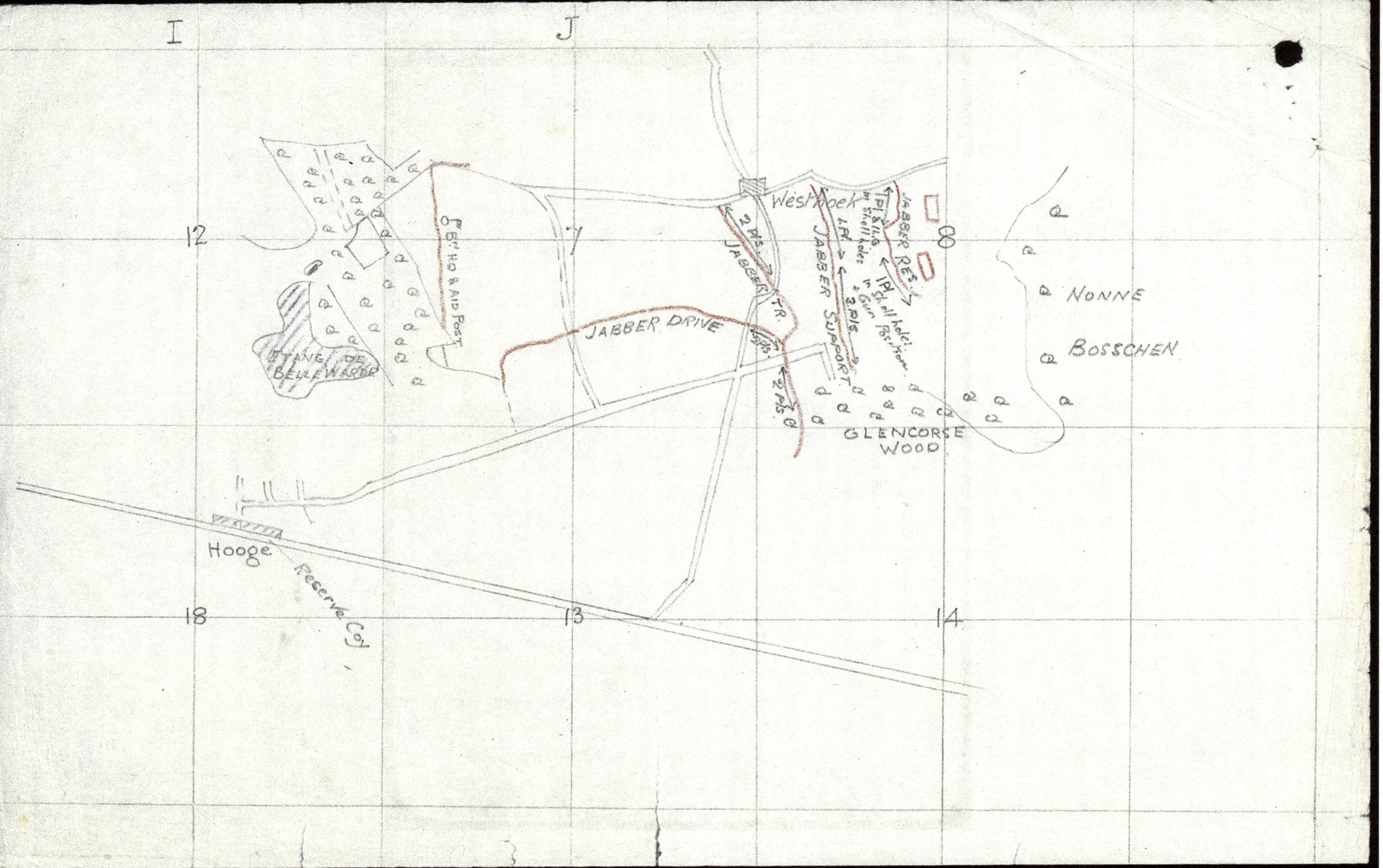
I
J
12
18
13
14
Westhoek
JABBER RES.
1 Pl & L.G. in Shell holes
1 Pl in Shell holes + Gun Position
1 Pl
2 Pls.
JABBER SUPPORT.
2 Pls.
JABBER TR.
2 Pls.
JABBER DRIVE
NONNE BOSSCHEN
GLENCORSE WOOD
Bn. HQ & AID POST
ETANG DE BELLEWAARDE
Hooge
Reserve Coy

1:10,000
Battery Positions (Possible strong points)
Probably Timber or Camouflage
Probably Concrete
HOOGE
EDITION 3
Zonnebeke
Square Fm
Low Fm
Vampir
Grey Ruin
Frost House
30
25
26
27
28
St Joseph's Inst.
Mühle
Brick Kiln & Yard
Tokio
Potsdam
Frezenberg
Rupprecht Fm
Bavaria Ho.
Railway Dump
C
D
I
J
Verlorenhoek
Bill Cottage
Douglas Villa
North Station Buildings
Halt
Rabbit Villa
South Station Buildings
Sans Souci
Albania
Helles
Anzac
Wilde Wood
Beckton Ho.
The Chapel
The Rectory
Oskar Fm
6
1
2
3
4
Kit & Kat
Cemetery
Red Lodge
NOTE
RIGHT BATT.
SUPPORT BATT.
Lake Fm
1 Coy.
Zig
Westhoek
Polygoneveld
Sieben Ho.
12
7
8
9
10
2 Coys.
1 Coy.
1 Comp.
Bellewaarde Fm
Nonne
Polygone Beek
Polygone de Zonnebeke
Y. Wood
Wee Cottages
BOUNDARY
DIV. BDY.
Bosschen
Chateau
Chateau Wood
The Culvert
Wing Ho.
Glencorse Wood
Black Watch Corner
Cameron Ho.
Hooge
1 COY
Verbeek Fm
Lone Ho.
Carlisle Fm
Surbiton Villas
18
13
14
15
16
Clapham Junction
Fitzclarence Fm
Northampton Fm
Zouave Wood
Inverness Copse
Polderhoek
Stirling Castle
Veldhoek
Herenthage Chât.
Kantinje Cab.
Dumbarton Lakes
Maple Copse
24
19
20
21
22
Godmin Copse
Tower Hamlets
Observatory Ridge
Rudkin Ho.
Clonmel Copse
Gheluvelt
Hat Pappotje Fm
Armagh Wood
Armagh Ho.
Lower Star Post
Scale: 1:10,000.
GERMAN TRENCHES CORRECTED FROM INFORMATION RECEIVED UP TO 13-8-17.
Machine Gun
Trench Mortar
Ammunition Dump
Supply Dump
Listening Post
Observation Post
Buried Cable

Copy No. 10

Training.

(1) During the forthcoming period out of the line the Brigadier General wishes every available effort to be devoted to the training of young officers and N.C.O.s with a view to preparing them as instructors for the reception of [illegible] drafts.

(2) Classes as under will be formed in Bns for the purpose:–

(a) Class for young Officers under the 2nd in Command

(b) " " N.C.O's " " Adjt. & R.S.M.

(3) The following subjects will be taught:–

(a) Elementary Field Fortification, comprising

(i) Working parties – method of filing on to & taking up tools & extending for work – using pick and shovel.

(ii) Wiring – Special attention is drawn to wiring drill on attached sheet.

Building dug-outs and shelter proofs against rifle grenades.

(iv) Siting & [illegible] revetting & building traverses.

(b) Bombing – use & method of handling Mills grenades – bomb throwing and the principle of the bomb attack.

(c) Musketry – This should include method of instruction on the range. Triangle of error & elementary tests for aiming and trigger pressing – rapid loading and firing.

(d) Close order drill and handling arms – The highest standard of personal efficiency and smartness in this subject must be expected from all young officers and N.C.O.s who are to be employed as instructors for drafts.

(4) The time out of the line should also be utilised in bringing Bn specialists up to establishment.

(5) All men, including if possible every employed man, should perform at least one hour's close order drill every day.

Physical exercises should also be practised.

(sd.) R. F. Foster
Major
Bde. Major
[illegible] Infantry Bde.

Copy No. 1 to O.C. No. 1 Coy.
" " 2 " " " 2 "
" " 3 " " " 3 "
" " 4 " " " 4 "
" " 5 " L.G. Officer
" " 6 " Bombing Officer
" " 7 }
" " 8 } Spare.
" " 9 }
" 10 War Diary.

355

SCHEDULE.

Unit	Unit relieved	Date	Time of arrival in new area.	New Billeting area	Remarks
6th Bn. Lond. Regt.	20th Bn. Lond. Regt.	2nd April	6 p.m.	VILLERS AU BOIS	
7th do.	(19th do. (18th do.	1st do. 2nd do.	11 a.m. ---	BOUVIGNY HUTS LORETTE TRENCHES	
8th do.	20th do.	2nd do.	1 p.m.	GOUY SERVINS	
15th do.	7th do.	2nd do.	6 p.m.	BOUVIGNY HUTS	

NOTE:- Guides for LORETTE Trenches will meet 7th Bn. London Regiment at the old Brigade Headquarters, ABLAIN, at 8.30 p.m.

356

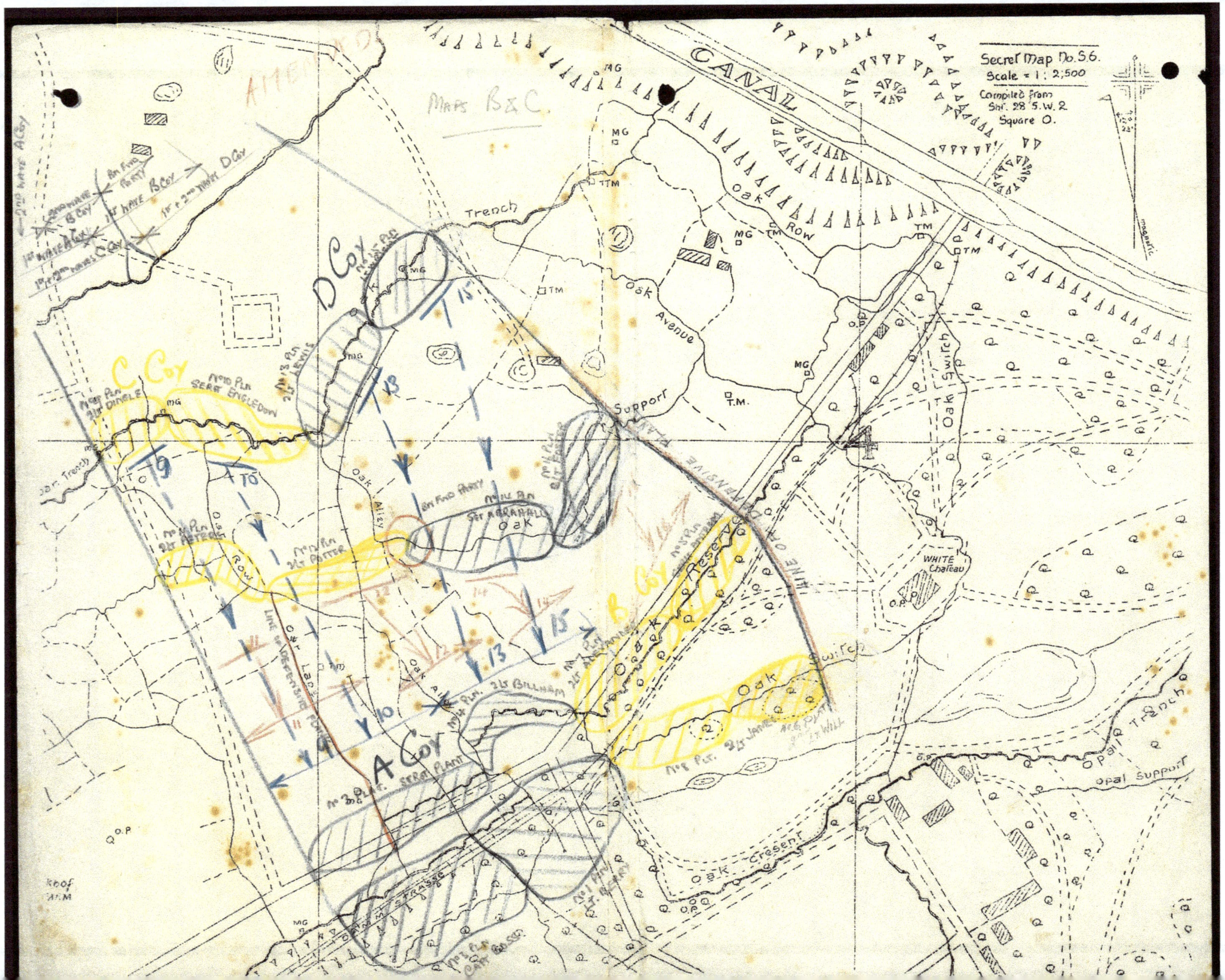

Secret Map No. 56.
Scale = 1 : 2,500
Compiled from
Sht. 28 S.W. 2
Square O.
magnetic
CANAL
Oak Row
Oak Avenue
Trench
Support
Oak Switch
Oak Alley
Oak Lane
Oak Reserve
Oak Cresent
Opal Trench
Opal Support
WHITE Chateau
LINE OF DEFENSIVE FLANK
Maps B & C
A Coy
B Coy
C Coy
D Coy
Row
Oak

Instructions regarding War Diaries and Intelligence Summaries are contained in F. S. Regs., Part II. and the Staff Manual respectively. Title Pages will be prepared in manuscript.

WAR DIARY

~~or~~

~~INTELLIGENCE SUMMARY~~

(Erase heading not required.)

Army Form C. 2118.

8th Batt London Regt R 140/47

Vol 32

Place	Date 1917	Hour	Summary of Events and Information	Remarks and references to Appendices
Support in GAVRELLE Sector	Oct 1-2		Battalion remained in support in GAVRELLE sector.	
BEVERLEY CAMP	3		Battalion relieved by 1/17th Bn. London Regt & moved to BEVERLEY CAMP.	
	4		Sec. Lt. CANCELLOR joined Battalion from Reserve 8th Battalion.	
	5		Sec. Lt. JAMES rejoined Battalion from Reserve 8th Battalion. Draft 4 O.Rs received.	
MAROEUIL	7		Battalion moved to billets at MAROEUIL.	
Left of OPPY Sector	10		Battalion relieved 1/21st London Regt in the front line on left of OPPY sector. Major WOOLLEY, 24th London joined Battalion.	
	11		Gas was projected by Special Coy. R.E. against enemy positions in and round OPPY. 700 rounds were fired and many casualties believed caused. Our casualties 1 O.R. Killed (gas), 1 O.R. wounded, 5 O.Rs wounded (gas).	
	12		A German wandered into our lines on A. Coy. front and was made prisoner. He was on a ration carrying fatigue and had lost his way. Much valuable information was obtained from him. A German patrol raided one of B. Coy's Lewis Gun posts and succeeded in capturing the gun. The Corporal in charge of the gun was wounded by a bomb. Casualties 1 O.R. Killed, 2 O.Rs wounded.	
	14		Two notice boards were erected in No Man's Land on night 14/15th. A notice in POLISH was inscribed on these boards "If you come over to us you will be well treated"	
	15		Casualties - 1 O.R. Killed, 2 O.Rs wounded.	

360

Instructions regarding War Diaries and Intelligence Summaries are contained in F. S. Regs., Part II. and the Staff Manual respectively. Title Pages will be prepared in manuscript.

WAR DIARY
or
~~INTELLIGENCE SUMMARY~~
(Erase heading not required.)

Army Form C. 2118.

Place	Date 1917	Hour	Summary of Events and Information	Remarks and references to Appendices
	Oct 16		Casualties - 2 O.Rs wounded.	
	17		Draft - 7 O.Rs received.	
Reserve at RAILWAY CUTTING	18		Battalion relieved by 6th London and moved into RESERVE at RAILWAY CUTTING.	
	23		Draft - 4 O.Rs received.	
	25		At 1.40 a.m. a fighting patrol consisting of Sec. Lt. FRYER, Sgt. WARE and 30 O.Rs B. Coy. raided enemy works at CRUCIFIX CORNER near OPPY under cover of a slight barrage. The position was found to be unoccupied by the enemy and was in a poor state of defence. Casualties - 3 O.Rs wounded.	
MAROEUIL	26		Battalion was relieved by 1/17th London Regt. and moved by lorries to billets at MAROEUIL.	
	27		Draft of 3 O.Rs received.	
	28		Capt. L.T. WHELAN, M.C., R.A.M.C., left the Battalion after 2½ years' continuous service to join No 39 Stationary Hospital. Capt. GOZNEY, M.C., assumed temporarily the medical charge of the Battalion.	
	30		Draft of 8 O.Rs received.	

[signature]
O/c 1/8th Bn London Regt
(Post Office Rifles)

BV/2464

2449 Wt. W14957/M90 750,000 1/16 J.B.C. & A. Forms/C.2118/12.

361

Instructions regarding War Diaries and Intelligence Summaries are contained in F. S. Regs., Part II. and the Staff Manual respectively. Title pages will be prepared in manuscript.

WAR DIARY
or
INTELLIGENCE SUMMARY.
(*Erase heading not required.*)

Army Form C. 2118.

1/8 London Regt
Vol 33

Place	Date	Hour	Summary of Events and Information	Remarks and references to Appendices
MAROEUIL	1917 Nov. 1		Lieutenant H. E. KEELY of the United States Medical Corps joined the Battalion as M.O.	EYW
	5th		The 140th Brigade relieved the 142nd Bde in the Right subsector of the Divisional sector, the Battalion going into support.	
			Dispositions A + B. Coys REDLINE.	
			C + D Coys NAVAL TRENCH.	EYW
			H.Q. do.	
			During the period in support the Battalion found the following working parties:	
			2 Coys for work in the front line. 1 Coy wiring in GAVRELLE. 1 Coy for work in THAMES STREET.	
	7th		Lt Col W. B. Vince M.C. proceeded on leave & Major Woolley took over command	EYW
	8th		Reinforcements 3 Officers (2nd Lieuts BISHOP, JOYCE, & McLEAN) + 1 O.R.	EYW
	9th		The Battalion relieved the 6th Battn in the GAVRELLE section this morning	EYW

A6945 Wt. W11422/M1160 35,000 12/16 D. D. & L. Forms/C./2118/14.

362

Instructions regarding War Diaries and Intelligence Summaries are contained in F. S. Regs., Part II. and the Staff Manual respectively. Title pages will be prepared in manuscript.

WAR DIARY
or
INTELLIGENCE SUMMARY.
(*Erase heading not required.*)

Army Form C. 2118.

Place	Date	Hour	Summary of Events and Information	Remarks and references to Appendices
	1917. Nov. 9th		Dispositions — Front Line: C & D Coys. Support: { A Coy less two platoons CECIL SUPPORT. / A Coy – 2 platoons RAILWAY TRENCH. } Reserve: B. Coy. MARINE TRENCH.	
		11.30am	Relief reported complete.	E.J.W.
			Between 10.30am & 2.30pm the enemy heavily shelled our trenches in the vicinity of MILL POST with all calibres. No casualties were caused.	
			The Major General visited the line this afternoon.	
			Reinforcements 2. ORs.	
	11th		This afternoon A Coy relieved C Coy who proceeded into ~~Reserve~~ support. B Coy relieved D Coy who proceeded into Reserve.	E.J.W.
			Casualty. 1. OR wounded.	
	12th		This afternoon the enemy shelled our support area with 5.9s & 4.2s about 100 shells in all fell. Reinforcement 1 Officer. (2nd Lt HIGGERTY.)	E.J.W.

A6945 Wt. W11422/M1160 350,000 12/16 D. D. & L. Forms/C./2118/14.

363

Army Form C. 2118.

Instructions regarding War Diaries and Intelligence Summaries are contained in F. S. Regs., Part II. and the Staff Manual respectively. Title pages will be prepared in manuscript.

WAR DIARY
or
INTELLIGENCE SUMMARY.
(*Erase heading not required.*)

Place	Date	Hour	Summary of Events and Information	Remarks and references to Appendices
	1917 Nov. 13th		The Battalion was relieved tonight by the 23rd London Regt. On completion of relief the Battalion moved back to WAKEFIELD CAMP.	EJW.
	14th		Reinforcement 6. ORs.	
	15th		Trench strength 23 Officers 553 ORs. Ration strength 25 do 673 ORs.	EJW
	16th		Reinforcement 1. OR. Casualty: Capt Johnson sent to hospital gassed.	EJW.
	18th		The Battalion relieved by 11th East YORKS + on completion of relief moved back into corps reserve at MONT ST ELOY.	EJW.
	21st		The Brigade moved to the HABARCQ area today. The Battalion marched at 8.30 am + billeted in HABARCQ.	

A6945 Wt. W11422/M1160 350,000 12/16 D. D. & L. Forms/C./2118/14.

364

Army Form C. 2118.

Instructions regarding War Diaries and Intelligence Summaries are contained in F. S. Regs., Part II. and the Staff Manual respectively. Title pages will be prepared in manuscript.

WAR DIARY
or
INTELLIGENCE SUMMARY.
(*Erase heading not required.*)

Place	Date	Hour	Summary of Events and Information	Remarks and references to Appendices
	1917 Nov. 22		The Brigade moved again today to the WANQUETIN area. The Battalion marched at 9.30am to billets in SIMENCOURT. Reinforcement 1 Officer (Lt CAUSTON) & 47 ORs.	EYW
	23rd		The Commanding Officer returned from leave & assumed command.	EYW
	24th		The Bde moved again today, the Battalion marching at 9.30am to billets in COURCELLES LES COMTE.	
	25th		The Battalion moved today at 1.40pm & marched via BAPAUME to camp opposite sugar factory at LETRANSLOY. Reinforcement 2 ORs.	EYW
	27th		At 2.30pm the Battalion moved by motor lorries to LEBOUQUIERES thence by march route to DOIGNIES where the Battn bivouaced for the night	EYW

A6945 Wt. W11422/M1160 350,000 12/16 D. D. & L. Forms/C./2118/14.

365

Army Form C. 2118.

WAR DIARY
or
INTELLIGENCE SUMMARY

(Erase heading not required.)

Instructions regarding War Diaries and Intelligence Summaries are contained in F. S. Regs., Part II. and the Staff Manual respectively. Title Pages will be prepared in manuscript.

Place	Date	Hour	Summary of Events and Information	Remarks and references to Appendices
	1917. Nov. 28th		The Battalion moved forward this morning into the Battle area + took up positions in reserve in the HINDENBURG LINE, in squares K.9. a + c. In the evening the Battalion took up fresh positions in the HINDENBURG SUPPORT LINE in squares K.4. d + K.10.b. (Reference: MOEUVRES 1/20000 Ed 5F)	EYW
	29th		Battalion remained in the HINDENBURG SUPPORT LINE.	
	30th		about 7a.m. the enemy started to shell in the neighbourhood of Bn. Hqrs. Soon after this, our guns opened, and it was clear that there was an enemy attack impendending. At about 9a.m. the Bn. was informed that the enemy had been seen massing behind BOURLON WOOD and in BOURLON VILLAGE, and that we must be prepared to go up and reinforce the front line, which was being held by the 6th Bn. and 15th Bn. At 11.30 AM orders were received to move 2 Coys. to the main CAMBRAI RD between ANNEUX CHAPEL and the SUGAR FACTORY and 2 Coys. and Bn. Hqrs. to a bank in a field just W. of GRAINCOURT village in E 29a. Accordingly the Bn. moved at 12 noon, A + B Coys. to the main Road and C + D Coys. to the bank. Bn. Hqrs. was established at about E 30c 26. The enemy was putting down a very heavy barrage W. of GRAINCOURT, and the Bn. suffered about 40 casualties, including 2nd Lt	

2449 Wt. W14957/M90 750,000 1/16 J.B.C. & A. Forms/C.2118/12.

PLAYFOOT

366

Army Form C. 2118.

Instructions regarding War Diaries and Intelligence Summaries are contained in F. S. Regs., Part II. and the Staff Manual respectively. Title Pages will be prepared in manuscript.

WAR DIARY
or
INTELLIGENCE SUMMARY
(Erase heading not required.)

Place	Date	Hour	Summary of Events and Information	Remarks and references to Appendices
	1917 Nov 30th		PLAYFOOT wounded, in passing through this. At about 12·40 orders were received that a Coy. was to be sent up to the SUNKEN ROAD running S.E through E24a to help the 6th Bn. A Coy. accordingly moved from the CAMBRAI RD at 1.30, and arrived just in time to co-operate with the reserve Coy of the 6th Bn. and counter-attack under Major Neely of the 6th Bn. This counter-attack was carried out with great dash and was entirely successful in stopping the German advance; and A Coy. dug in about 300 yds. behind our original front line. Orders were then received for the remainder of the Bn. to move up to the slope W. of BOURLON WOOD and support the 6th and 15th Bns. The Coys. moved at 2·30 and were in position about 3.30 p.m. When Bn Hqrs. arrived, it was found that the 15th were still holding their original line on the crest in the wood, but that the 6th had been forced to give way and had suffered very heavy casualties. Accordingly B and D Coys. were sent up on either side of the SUNK RD running N. in E18c. to clear up the situation and to connect A Coy with the defensive flank held by the 15th Bn along	

2449 Wt. W14957/M90 750,000 1/16 J.B.C. & A. Forms/C.2118/12.

367

Army Form C. 2118.

WAR DIARY
or
INTELLIGENCE SUMMARY
(Erase heading not required.)

Instructions regarding War Diaries and Intelligence Summaries are contained in F. S. Regs., Part II. and the Staff Manual respectively. Title Pages will be prepared in manuscript.

Place	Date	Hour	Summary of Events and Information	Remarks and references to Appendices
	1917 Nov. 13th		along the edge of the wood. This was done just before dark, and the line then ran from about E 17 d 5 5 across the SUNKEN RD to edge of wood at about E 18 c 9 7. Bn Hqrs. was established in the 15th Bn. Hqrs. at about E 24 b. 8 6.	
			C Coy. was placed at the disposal of the 15th Bn., two platoons being sent to support the front line, and 2 platoons being held in reserve near Bn Hqrs. This Coy did exceedingly good work in carrying up ammunition and rations and was specially thanked by the O.C 15th Bn.	
			The situation remained unchanged until after midnight.	
			Casualties. It is difficult to state exactly our casualties on this day, as the Bn. continued in action for 3 days, and the casualties were taken as a whole for the four days. A Coy. lost about 40 in their counter-attack (2/Lt Bishop Killed). The other Coys. suffered slight casualties, 2Lt Higgerty (D) wounded and	

2449 Wt. W14957/M90 750,000 1/16 J.B.C. & A. Forms/C.2118/12.

368

Army Form C. 2118.

Instructions regarding War Diaries and Intelligence Summaries are contained in F. S. Regs., Part II. and the Staff Manual respectively. Title Pages will be prepared in manuscript.

WAR DIARY
or
INTELLIGENCE SUMMARY

(Erase heading not required.)

Place	Date	Hour	Summary of Events and Information	Remarks and references to Appendices
	1917 Nov. 30th		and missing. (This officer went out on a patrol up the SUNKEN ROAD, was seen to be wounded, and did not return) 2Lt FRYER (B) wounded. (Reference BOURLON 1/10000)	

[signature] Lt Col

O/c 1/8th Bn London Regt.

(Post Office Rifles)

2449 Wt. W14957/M90 750,000 1/16 J.B.C. & A. Forms/C.2118/12.

369

Headquarters
140th Infantry Brigade

Herewith War Diary for month of
December 1917

[signature]
Lt Col
B.V. 778
4-1-1918
Cmdg 8th London Regt.

OVE

370

Instructions regarding War Diaries and Intelligence Summaries are contained in F. S. Regs., Part II. and the Staff Manual respectively. Title Pages will be prepared in manuscript.

WAR DIARY
or
INTELLIGENCE SUMMARY
(Erase heading not required.)

Army Form C. 2118.

140/47 1/8 London Regt Vol 34

Place	Date	Hour	Summary of Events and Information	Remarks and references to Appendices
BOURLON WOOD Sunken Rd.	Dec. 1st		Very early this morning the 7th Batt London Regt came up and relieved what was left of the 6th Batt and A & B Coys who were on the left of the Sunken Rd. running through E.18.a & c.	
			B Coy. moved across the road on the right of D Coy. and held up to the edge of the wood. A Coy. came back into support in the Sunken Road.	
			There was no activity during the day beyond a certain amount of sniping and Machine Gun fire.	
			At night the 15th Batt on our right and our C Coy. were relieved by the 21st Batt. and C Coy. came back to the Sunken Road.	
			The next day was also quiet. At midday O.Cs 7th & 8th Batts were sent for to Brigade H.Q. and ordered to make an attack that night to regain the high ground under cover of an artillery barrage.	
	Dec. 2nd		The attack was made at 8.10pm. the 8th Bn. being on the right from the edge of the wood to the Sunken Road (inclusive) with the 7th Batt on the left.	
			The attack was made with A Coy. on the right and C Coy. on the left. A platoon of D Coy. was placed under the orders of O.C. C Coy. for the purpose of clearing the Sunken Road & keeping touch with the 7th	
			The attack was extremely successful. No organised enemy line was encountered, although there was some fighting with parties of the enemy who were in shell holes.	
			On reaching the objective the two Coys. were reinforced by two platoons of B Coy. and 1 platoon of the 21st Batt. and dug in a line from the left of the 21st just behind our original front line up to the bend in the Sunken Road at E.18.a.5.3.	
			Thence the line ran down the Sunken Road for about 150 yards where it	

2449 Wt. W14957/M90 750,000 1/16 J.B.C. & A. Forms/C.2118/12.

371

Army Form C. 2118.

WAR DIARY
or
INTELLIGENCE SUMMARY

(Erase heading not required.)

Instructions regarding War Diaries and Intelligence Summaries are contained in F. S. Regs., Part II. and the Staff Manual respectively. Title Pages will be prepared in manuscript.

Place	Date	Hour	Summary of Events and Information	Remarks and references to Appendices
	Dec. 2nd (contd)		joined the right of the 7th Bn. The enemy appears to have been taken entirely by surprise. This was subsequently confirmed by prisoners' statements. We advanced about 300 to 400 yards and captured 30 prisoners and 9 machine guns. Our casualties were 2 Officers & 30 O.Rs.	
			At 11 pm a Company of the R.W.F. came up to the new front line & assisted in the consolidation. This Company worked splendidly and was of the very greatest assistance to the Battn.	
	Dec. 3rd		The situation remained unchanged, and in the evening the Battn was relieved by the 23rd Lond. Reg. and on completion of the relief marched back to trenches in K.21.a.	
			The casualties for the 4 days were as follows:- Officers. Killed 1, Missing 1, Wounded 5. O.Rs Killed 23, Missing 21, Died of wounds 11, Wounded 122. Officers' casualties - Killed - 2/Lt P.S. Bishop, Missing 2/Lt J.C. Haggerty, Wounded, 2/Lts J.L. Playfoot, B.J. Dyer, R. Hainsworth, J.S. McKenzie and E.W. Miles.	
HINDENBURG SUPPORT LINE	Dec. 4th		This afternoon the Battn moved forward to the HINDENBURG SUPPORT LINE in K.16.b & d. Dispositions D Coy Right Front B " Left " C " Right Support A " Left " News comes that the Army is evacuating the forward positions and retiring to the HINDENBURG SUPPORT LINE. Retirement started at 3 am 5th inst.	

372

Army Form C. 2118.

Instructions regarding War Diaries and Intelligence Summaries are contained in F. S. Regs., Part II. and the Staff Manual respectively. Title Pages will be prepared in manuscript.

WAR DIARY
or
INTELLIGENCE SUMMARY
(Erase heading not required.)

Place	Date	Hour	Summary of Events and Information	Remarks and references to Appendices
	Dec. 5th		The withdrawal began at 3am and last troops left at 4am. Germans were seen on the ridge at about 11 am. The Battn moved into trenches in K.17.c. with H.Q. at K.15.d.9.9. Reinforcement 3 O.Rs	
	Dec 6th		Casualty - 1 O.R. wounded.	
	Dec 7th		The Battn relieved by 7th Battn and moved back to trenches in K.21.c. Casualties - Killed 1, Died of wounds 2, Wounded 4.	
	Dec 8th		Casualty 1 O.R. wounded.	
	Dec 10th		Capt. L.E.B. Jacob proceeded on leave and 2/Lt Potter took the place of Adjutant. The Battn. dug a new support line during the night behind HUGHES SWITCH in K.16.a and K.15.b. (Ref. MOEUVRES MAP 1/20000). Reinforcement 1 Officer (Lt MALLISON) + 1 O.R.	
BERTINCOURT	Dec 11th		The Battn relieved by 24th Battn and moved back into Divisional relief at BERTINCOURT.	
	Dec 13th		Reinforcement 1 O.R.	
HINDENBURG SUPPORT TRENCH.	Dec 15th		The Battn proceeded to the front line and relieved 2 Coys 22nd Lond Reg. + 2 Coys. of Composite Battn of 141st Bde. Relief complete at 10.45pm. During this time the Bde. is attached to 59th Division. Dispositions - C Coy. Front line posts in K.10.d. + K.11.c. A.B. and D Coys in HINDENBURG SUPPORT TRENCH. Trench strength - 20 Officers, 540 O.Rs.	

2449 Wt. W14957/M90 750,000 1/16 J.B.C. & A. Forms/C.2118/12.

373

Army Form C. 2118.

WAR DIARY
or
INTELLIGENCE SUMMARY
(Erase heading not required.)

Instructions regarding War Diaries and Intelligence Summaries are contained in F. S. Regs., Part II. and the Staff Manual respectively. Title Pages will be prepared in manuscript.

Place	Date	Hour	Summary of Events and Information	Remarks and references to Appendices
	Dec. 16th		The Battn dug a new front line from K.10.d.5.9 to K.11.c.8.7. approx. in conjunction with the R.W.F. and also a support line 200 yds behind. This work was continued during the whole time. Casualty 1 O.R. wounded.	
	Dec. 18th		Reinforcement - 4 O.Rs	
	Dec. 19th		The new front line was occupied today along its whole length as follows:- 3 platoons of C Coy. & 1 platoon of A with 7 Lewis Guns. Reinforcement - 25 O.Rs	
BERTINCOURT	Dec. 21st		Battn relieved by the 8th Battn South Staffs & on completion of relief moved back to BERTINCOURT.	
MERICOURT	Dec. 22nd		The Battn. marched to YTRES where it entrained for MERICOURT, arriving late at night. The Division is now in Army Reserve.	
	Dec. 31st		Under authority granted by H.M. The King, the undermentioned N.C.Os & men have been awarded the MILITARY MEDAL by the Corps Commander for gallantry during the recent operations:- Sergts T.L. COUGHLIN, P.J. JAGO, C.E. HORROCKS, & C.E. CLARK, Corpl T.H. PERRY, L/Corps A. PEPPERELL, S. VOCKINS, & G.W. MACKAY, Riflemen H.B. JEPHCOTT, F. COLEMAN, C.G. COPPIN, A. TREEBY, C. EDWARDS, T.H. SUGGARS, E. HAAGMAN, & F.R. SHELDON.	

B. Vince
Lt-Col
Comdg 1/8th Battn London Regt
(Post Office Rifles).

Instructions regarding War Diaries and Intelligence Summaries are contained in F. S. Regs., Part II. and the Staff Manual respectively. Title pages will be prepared in manuscript.

WAR DIARY
or
INTELLIGENCE SUMMARY.
(Erase heading not required.)

140/47

1/8 London Regt

Vol 35

Army Form C. 2118.

Place	Date	Hour	Summary of Events and Information	Remarks and references to Appendices
	Jan		Battalion at MERICOURT L'ABBE.	
	1		The following New Year Honours were granted to the Battalion.	
			Capt. & Qmr. R. Fairley M.C.	
			CSM. H.M. Turner M.C.	
			Capt & Adj[t] L.E.B. Jacob } Mentioned in Despatches	
			CSM. A.G. Richardson }	
	2		Bn at MERICOURT	
			2/Lt. Simpson 21st London Regt joined Bn temporarily.	
	3-9		Bn at MERICOURT	
	10		Bn moved by train to BERTINCOURT	
	11		Bn. at BERTINCOURT	
	12		Bn relieved 1/23rd London in left section of RIBECOURT sub-sector.	
	13-14		Bn holding the line Casualties 2 ORs wounded	
	15		do Ration Strength 19-575 Trench Strength 16-420.	
			Casualties 3 OR killed 1 OR wounded	
	16		Bn relieved by 1/15th London Regt and moved into support in RIBECOURT village	

A5834 Wt. W4973 M687 750,000 8/16 D. D. & L. Ltd. Forms/C.2118/13.

Instructions regarding War Diaries and Intelligence Summaries are contained in F. S. Regs., Part II. and the Staff Manual respectively. Title pages will be prepared in manuscript.

WAR DIARY
or
INTELLIGENCE SUMMARY.
(Erase heading not required.)

Army Form C. 2118.

Place	Date	Hour	Summary of Events and Information	Remarks and references to Appendices
	Jan 17-18		Bn in RIBECOURT	
	19		Bn relieved 1/6th Londn Regt in centre section of RIBECOURT sub sector.	
	20-23		Bn holding the line. Casualty 1 O.R. wounded	
	24		Bn relieved by 1/18th Londn Regt and moved to BERTINCOURT. Casualty 1 O.R. wounded	
	25		Bn in BERTINCOURT. Major E. J. Woolley M.C. left Bn and joined 1/15th Londn Regt	
	26		Bn in BERTINCOURT Draft 51 O.Rs.	
	27		do do. G.O.C. 47th Divn presented Medal Ribbons to officers & men of the Bn at Brigade Church Parade	
	28.		Orders were received to disband the Battalion.	
	30		7 Officers and 250 men sent to 1/24th Londn Regt	
	31		8 Officers and 300 men sent to 1/17th Londn Regt. Headquarters and 200 men ~~sent~~ posted to 2/8th Londn Regt with orders to proceed to that Battalion on the 2nd Feb. So ends the career of the 1/8th Battalion The London Regt (T F) The Post Office Rifles, after 2 years and 10 months service in France	

A5834 Wt. W4973 M687 750,000 8/16 D. D. & L. Ltd. Forms/C.2118/13.

376

Army Form C. 2[illegible]

Instructions regarding War Diaries and Intelligence Summaries are contained in F. S. Regs., Part II. and the Staff Manual respectively. Title pages will be prepared in manuscript.

WAR DIARY
or
INTELLIGENCE SUMMARY.

(Erase heading not required.)

Place	Date	Hour	Summary of Events and Information	Remarks and references to Appendices
	Jan 31		with the 140th Brigade of the 47th (London) Division.	
			The Battalion landed in France on the 17th of March 1915. During its career it took part in the following engagements.	
			FESTUBERT May 1915	
			LOOS Sept 1915	
			VIMY RIDGE May 1916	
			SOMME BATTLE:	
			Operations in HIGH WOOD and beyond Sept 1916	
			Operations near BUTTE DE WARLENCOURT Oct 1916	
			MESSINES June 1917	
			BOURLON WOOD Nov. and Dec. 1917	
			The Battalion is gone, and its officers and men scattered abroad. But the spirit of the Battalion — that same spirit which carried it through over 2½ years of hard fighting — will always remain in the hearts of all those who have served in and for it. "Olim meminisse iuvabit".	
			[illegible] Lt Col Cdg 1/8th London Regt 1/2/18	

A5834 Wt. W4973 M687 750,000 8/16 D. D. & L. Ltd. Forms/C.2118/13.

377

www.ingramcontent.com/pod-product-compliance
Lightning Source LLC
Chambersburg PA
CBHW081527160426
43191CB00011B/1699
9781474526302